INTRODUCTION

Everybody wants people to like them. I've never met someone who didn't. They don't always admit it. Some people want it more than others, but all of us want to be seen, known, and loved. We want friends.

We want to win with people.

This isn't easy for pastors. People are complicated. They're busy. They get caught up in their feelings. Most of the time they struggle to even articulate their emotions. You're trying to serve them, but suddenly they blow up on you.

You're thinking, *Where did that come from?* You're not even sure what they're talking about. But it makes more sense later when you learn their issue didn't have anything to do with you. You just happened to be there so you were on the receiving end of their pain and frustration.

It can be difficult not to take this personally.

I didn't understand all of this when I first started in ministry. I was young when I started. I was a twenty-one-year-old senior pastor. I was not a good one. And the people weren't afraid to tell me!

My problem was not a lack of effort. I wore a three-piece suit in a school cafetorium because I thought it could make me more respectable.

I preached my heart out, which usually led to profuse sweating. I was so passionate about what I was saying, I'd prowl back and forth like a panther.

There were many weekends where I felt inadequate. I didn't know if the message and the service were good. Perhaps the bigger issue was, I didn't know if I was any good. I would get so ramped up. I had so much passion and fire—and so many words. I had thoughts on everything. It was usually about Jesus and about an hour!

But in those moments of prayerful preparation, Jesus always gave me the same reminder: *Jeff, make sure you tell them I love them.*

I remember those moments that happened decades ago like they were yesterday. I've thought about those words from Jesus every time I've preached since those days.

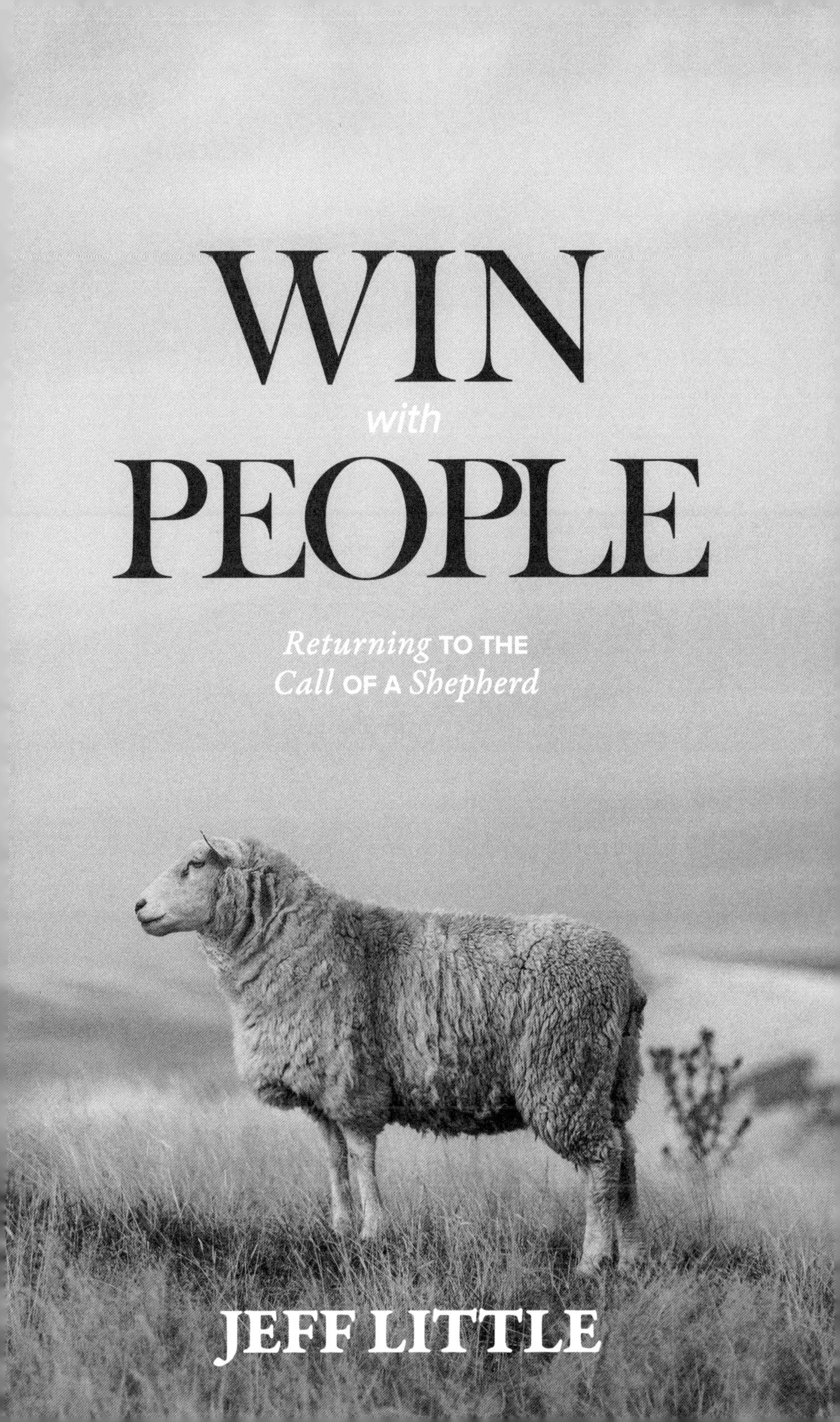
WIN
with
PEOPLE
Returning TO THE
Call OF A Shepherd
JEFF LITTLE

Win with People: Returning to the Call of a Shepherd

www.leadtowin.com
ISBN: 978-1-954961-20-3

Printed in the United States.

CONTENTS

Jeff, make sure you tell them I love them.

I'm grateful for my heritage that gave me a high view of Scripture. Because of this, I've always worked diligently to be faithful to God's Word, to present it in context, and to honor the historical interpretation and application.

I'm still committed to this approach, but what I realize now that I didn't then is that people don't remember most of what you say. They want to laugh and they like good stories. They want to learn the Bible and some of what we say sticks.

But what they really remember is what they felt. Especially when they feel God and His presence. They probably don't have the words to describe it, but it changes them.

This process led me to an important realization. I wanted my life to count. I wanted to change the world for the glory of God. I wanted to build His Kingdom and advance the mission of His Church.

I wanted to be "super . . ." I just wasn't sure what that meant.

Super . . . *star*?
Super . . . *leader*?
Super . . . *pastor*?

I was not going to draw tens of thousands regularly purely on my speaking ability or my profound insights. If I made that my focus and my ultimate goal, I was going to spend most of my time frustrated.

But I realized if I was going to be a "super" anything, my greatest potential was to be a "supercoach."

If I didn't focus on promoting myself and all of my talents and gifts but instead leveraged who God called me to be into helping and serving other people, my impact could extend far beyond my natural ability through the supernatural grace of God and His power moving through His people.

Coaches help their players get better. They develop them. They help them overcome obstacles and injuries. They prepare them for what's coming next. They give all they've got to help the team win.

The Bible has a word for "coach." It's the word "pastor." And in the New Testament, the word we translate as "pastor" (in the Greek, *poimén*) is the same word translated as "shepherd."

Maybe you've forgotten this. I want to call us back to this biblical pattern. A pastor is a coach. A pastor is a shepherd.

You may have a reaction to the term "shepherd." In certain leadership circles, this concept can be looked down upon.

From this perspective, sheep are viewed as gullible people and shepherds are seen as those responsible to watch out for small clusters of people who need extra help.

It's not uncommon for pastors who want to grow big churches to think about smaller environments when they hear the term "shepherd." They don't think about a shepherd who trains and develops teams of shepherds.

The phrase also fell out of favor during the early days of "The Church Growth Movement." That term refers to a movement in the late '70s and the early '80s, in which Donald McGavran, C. Peter Wagner, Lyle Schaller, and others drastically changed the way church leaders thought about church. They combined a renewed emphasis on discipleship and spiritual gifts with science and data to explore how churches could become more strategic and, as a result, grow larger.

Schaller argued that one of the things holding back smaller churches from growth is the inability to see themselves as not just shepherds of a small flock of sheep, but of other shepherds, cowboys, and ranch hands.

A shepherd who trains other shepherds, cowboys, and ranch hands is called a rancher. Ranchers love the sheep but they also manage the ranch. They delegate, which means they're not directly involved with the total care of every animal.[1]

Schaller was onto something. It's typical in smaller churches for the pastor to do everything and to take care of everyone. This keeps him so busy with a few needy people that he never has time to work on the things that could help the church grow. The Church Growth Model emphasizes that every person in the church joins the mission and offers their talents to serve the body. This is a biblical approach.

When Schaller challenged these pastors to spend less time taking care of everyone and to spend more time pastoring and discipling the people in the church so they would be capable of leading others, it provided a helpful strategy.

This is very similar to what the apostles did in Acts 6. They divided up the work and delegated food distribution and other pastoral tasks to free up the leaders to use their gifts.

Every pastor I know wants to learn how to make their church grow. They want to reach more people and expand their impact. They like the idea of becoming a rancher.

But you can't skip steps. This was never Schaller's point. You can't become a rancher if you've never been a shepherd. Ranchers know so much about sheep that they're the ones the shepherds turn to for help. That's how it's supposed to work.

Pastors can't skip the step of caring for people just to focus on managing a big church. That's not healthy for the church or the pastor.

We want our churches to grow and expand, but not at the

expense of the health of the people. Think about it like this: If we build big people, the people will build a big church. If we build big teams, the teams will be able to care for lots of sheep.

That's how we win with people. That's my dream for my church and for yours. I designed this book to help you, myself, and our teams return to this call of a shepherd so we can lead the sheep well.

I believe this honors God and motivates Him to entrust us with more sheep.

This book is for you *and* your team. My prayer is you will go through it together, and that through the process you will grow and get better.

It's simple. Healthy sheep reproduce and multiply. What if we asked ourselves a few questions as we get started:

Do I know what it means to shepherd the flock?

Do I care about the sheep or do I only care what the sheep can do for me?

Does my daily routine help the sheep get healthy?

What practical things could I do to help more sheep?

We don't have to choose one or the other. We can have large, growing churches that also genuinely care for the sheep.

It's possible.

Once, at our membership class I was talking to a room of several hundred people. Many of them had come from the service where I just preached. There was a single mom who wanted to explain how she felt.

She said, "I don't know you. I've never met you, but when I come here, I feel like you care. You're here with us." I responded by saying, "You feel like I care, because I do care! That's why I'm here in this room. I want to meet you. I want to shake your hand and hear your story. And I want you to know what our church is all about."

After this conversation, I thought about how low the bar has fallen for pastors—now you get credit for caring about your job and actually being at church with the people. That doesn't seem like a target that's too difficult to hit.

I want to take you on a journey to return to the biblical call of a shepherd. Anytime we go on a journey we want to know where we're headed.

So, here's a brief description of where we'll go together.

First, we will answer the question, **"Why Do We Need to Win with People?"** In other words, what's the point of this book? What does it mean to be called by God? How does that work? What does He call us to? Unfortunately, too many of us have missed it. We need to return to the call of a shepherd.

Second, we'll explore the idea, **"Shepherds Smell Like Sheep."** Jesus told us to feed His sheep. People are not an obstacle or a nuisance; they're what God cares about. To care for the people and help them on their journey, we've got to be with them.

Third, a shepherd is entrusted to care for the sheep. To do this well, we need **"God's Heart for People."** After all, they're His sheep. How we treat them is a reflection of our love for Him. We need to see them the way He does.

Fourth, we'll do a deep dive into the standard for all shepherds—Jesus Himself. We're His sheep; He's our Shepherd. How does He lead? When we answer His call, we become "undershepherds." We're apprenticing to learn the art of being a shepherd from **"Jesus, the Chief Shepherd."**

Fifth, all of the concepts up to this point speak to and benefit all followers of Christ. Learning to love people the way God loves them will help us no matter what we do professionally. But there's a difference for those who respond to a vocational call to ministry. How do we identify and follow **"The Call of the Shepherd's Life"**?

Sixth, now that I've made my case that we've been called to be shepherds, I want to get practical with you. How does this actually change what we do? I'll take you into the nuts and bolts as we consider **"Practical Ways Your Church Can Win with People."**

Seventh, both winning and losing are contagious. No one has more influence over the culture of an environment than the leader. If you want your church, your campus, your team, or your department to be a place where people win, you have to overcome **"The Shepherd's Most Important Challenge."**

Eighth, ministry is a team sport—the best flocks are led by teams of shepherds. A skilled and intentional team of shepherds can care for a lot of sheep. That's why it's vital you learn how to **"Win with Your Team."**

Ninth, a winning team is an expanding team. Growth and expansion come with new opportunities and new challenges. That's why you have to take the time to understand **"How to Help the Herd Win."**

Tenth, shepherds care for the sheep and comfort the flock when they're afraid. But there are moments when the shepherd has to fight to protect the sheep from predators. Great shepherds who win with people value **"Protecting Your Winning Culture."**

Eleventh, as we grow in our ability to win with people, the people expect us to get bigger. They want space for their friends and loved ones. They want to start a new program, a new initiative, or plant a new campus in their town. In order to do this, we need to understand how to think and lead like **"The Multi-Dimensional Shepherd."**

Finally, as we come to the end of the journey, we need clear action steps. Where do we start? What are the most important things we can do right now to get better? What are the next steps after that? What we really need is a clear plan that will help us **"Win Today, Win Tomorrow."**

It's an incredible privilege to go on this journey with you. I can't wait to get started.

Let's go!

CHAPTER ONE

WHY DO WE NEED TO WIN WITH PEOPLE?

"God has called you."

It sounds so spiritual and exciting. Because it comes from God, it's filled with the sense of purpose and destiny we're all longing for. Genuine fulfillment and significance are implied.

But what does it mean, and how does it work?

We like the idea that the Creator of the universe knows who we are, entrusts us with a mission, and has expectations for what our lives can become.

But it also comes with tremendous pressure.

- ***What if I make a wrong choice?***
- ***How do I know for sure?***
- ***What if I don't have what I need?***
- ***What if it feels like everyone else is further than I am?***
- ***What if I never get the opportunity to do what God's called me to do?***
- ***What if I don't have what it takes?***

You've probably experienced one or all of these feelings. We all have. These are not minor worries or anxieties. If we don't deal with them, they keep us up at night even after our head hits the pillow. They steal our joy. They rob our peace.

But we don't have to live here. We don't have to allow these toxic thoughts to keep us from becoming who God has called us to be. Your birthday is the day you enter the world. But your most exciting day is when you understand why.[1] That's why I wrote this book.

I want all of us to return to the purity and simplicity of what it means to be called by God and to discover the purpose He has for our lives.

Every follower of Christ is created by God with a purpose and is called to a holy life.[2] This is not for a privileged few.

Jesus built His entire strategy around empowering His followers to be His hands and feet in the earth. Every single one of us is born with a unique contribution and purpose to offer God as an act of worship.[3]

If you're a follower of Christ, you're in ministry. Your seat is not in the stands. He's given you a jersey. You're in the game.

However, if you're reading this book, there's a strong likelihood you're already in vocational ministry, or you're seriously considering it.

And I'm not just talking about senior pastors. That's my role, so I love and appreciate anyone willing to answer that call. It's not easy. Yes, it comes with some unique benefits, but it also carries extraordinary stress, pressure, and vulnerability.

However, I realize it's not the only position on the team. Great players may have impressive stats, and the legendary ones break historical records. But it takes a team to win a championship.

We have different responsibilities and positions on the team, but all of us are moving toward the same goal.

- **Maybe you serve on the connections team or lead volunteer teams.**

- **Maybe you work with youth or kids ministry.**
- **Maybe you are on the worship or production team.**
- **Maybe you work in the business office or you have an administrative role.**
- **Maybe you serve on a team or in an area I've never heard of.**

Here's what I want you to know: *your contribution matters.*

Read that again. God sees and honors your service. He receives it as holy.

You may find yourself on a team you didn't choose or expect. You might have a dream in your heart to serve on a different team. Or in a different place. Or at a different church.

Don't let the enemy lie to you. You're not the only person who's ever felt this way. Most ministry leaders wrestle with these thoughts. It doesn't mean you're in the wrong place, playing the wrong position, or stuck in this role for the rest of your life.

The promotion you're waiting for will not come from constantly looking for something better. It won't happen by networking and getting your name out there.

The Bible says promotion comes from the Lord.[4] He does it. He sees you and can open a door for you no person or challenging circumstance can shut. Keep being faithful where you are.

Keep giving your teammates and the people you're serving your absolute best effort.

Can I give you one practical tip as a pastor? If you're feeling this way, don't process down to younger or newer team members or sideways with your peers. Process up—talk to your manager or direct report. Be honest about what you're feeling. Have a good spirit. Listen to what they say. God honors this approach.

Remember, the enemy hates what you're doing. He never stops lying. He wants to drive a wedge between you and God. He wants to erode the trust between you and the team where you serve.

The Bible describes the enemy's strategy as a lion who prowls around looking for someone to devour.[5] We don't have to be afraid, but we need to be wise.

Ministry life is not the most comfortable career path. It can be a terrible job. I often say, "There are more lucrative ways to be miserable."

But when you've been called by God, there's nothing like it.

Technology has changed the way we think about ministry. When I first started, we didn't really know what everyone else was doing. We may have gone to a conference or an event once a year and heard a national speaker.

Today, we can watch, evaluate, and keep up with every church in our city, our region, our nation, and around the world. If we want to, we can keep up with everything that's happening in the big, diverse, multi-faceted body of Christ.

There may be value in having a greater understanding of other models. The downside is we can easily compare ourselves with everyone else. We put pressure on ourselves to be famous, to build big platforms, and to create large social brands.

We work really hard to build something that creates a little momentum, but the moment we compare ourselves to others, we end up feeling insignificant. To combat these feelings, we may try to go bigger and bolder. We think "production" and "spectacle." If we're not careful, we fall into the trap of trying to entertain people.

I realize we all use varying degrees of production. When we first started, we used an overhead projector and a basic sound system. Today we have LED walls, lights, cameras, tablets for the kids' check-in, and all kinds of tech our team convinced us we needed.

But these are tools. They're not the goal. When they help us to more effectively serve and love people and when they help people experience a genuine relationship with Jesus, they're valuable assets.

However, our production becomes a trap the moment we start to see ourselves primarily as a venue for live entertainment. We're not trying to compete with concert venues, fine dining, Netflix, or the NFL.

Have you ever felt the pressure to compete in that space? It's demoralizing because it feels like we can't win with the people. It's not what they're asking us to be. They don't need another entertainer—they need a pastor who will help them grow closer to God.

With all the content out there (podcasts, TED Talks, MasterClass, etc.), we also feel the expectation to come up with deep revelation and profound insights no one has ever heard before.

But I don't think it's what God expects from us. We're putting pressure on ourselves to be something He never asked us to be. And I don't think it's what the people we serve are expecting, either.

No matter what role we have or where we serve, trying to be something we're not saps our strength and puts us on the fast track toward burnout.

Let's come back to the simplicity and purity of what it means to be called by God.

Have you had that moment?

If so, go back to the moment when you said "Yes" to Jesus.

What are we actually called to? What did we say "Yes" to?

- **In the Bible, the words "pastor" and "shepherd" are used interchangeably.**
- **Psalms has more chapters than any other book in the Bible, and the most well-known psalm begins, "The Lord is my shepherd."[6]**
- **Multiple times in Psalms, God's people are described as His sheep, the people of His pasture.[7]**
- **Many of the key characters in the Old Testament took care of sheep—the list includes Abraham, Jacob, Joseph, Moses, David, and more.**
- **Jesus called Himself "The Good Shepherd."[8]**
- **Peter and Paul, the two most prominent leaders of the early church, remind us to live and act like shepherds.[9]**
- **You could say the Bible is a book about shepherds, often written BY shepherds.**

Today, people often think ministry means being a platform personality, an influencer, a conference speaker, or a dynamic leader. We may do some of these things, but they're not the primary goal.

The Bible says, "Be a shepherd."

This is where the idea for this book came from. It started in my own time with God. Then I shared it with our team. And then I began sharing it in other environments. To my surprise, the simplicity of this message really resonated with people—especially with those who had given their lives to vocational ministry.

My prayer is that God will use it to strengthen and inspire you.

Ministry is challenging. It's never finished. If you're looking for the sense of completion when you go home from work each day, you're going to be disappointed. Ministry comes with pressure no one sees. It's often lonely.

We make mistakes and feel shame. We're disappointed with unmet expectations. We wonder if there's something else we could be doing.

Another challenge we navigate is that we're not designed to do ministry alone. It's not good for us to be alone. Ecclesiastes 4:9 reminds us that two are better than one. It's easy to end up here, but if we asked Elijah, he would tell us it never goes well when we feel like we're the only ones.[10]

The call to ministry is the call to serve Jesus. We have preferences and opinions, but we serve Him.

Jesus calls each of us to ministry, but He also places us with other people. He sent the disciples out in pairs, not as lone rangers.[11] Having a partner or being on a team requires character because we care so much about what we're doing and teammates have opinions.

While it's often hard for us to recognize, the truth is, we live in the most individualistic society in the history of the world. We think "me," "my gifts," and "my opportunities." God's vision does not start with us. We're not at the center.

It's critical for all of us, no matter our role, to have a clear understanding of this pattern:

1. **God has a vision for a church.**
2. **He entrusts that vision to a leader who casts the vision to the people.**
3. **God calls people as a team to carry the vision.**

It may seem obvious or simple, but this kind of clarity is important.

First and foremost, because the vision belongs to God, all of us are serving Him. However, serving the vision also means supporting and serving the leader God entrusted to cast the vision.

This does not mean we mindlessly do whatever the leader

asks, but it does mean our starting place is, "How can I help? I'm grateful to be here! Let's do something great for the Kingdom!" Everyone wants to be on a team like that, but it starts with being that kind of team member.

For mature Christ followers, serving Jesus leads to serving your pastor, which leads to serving the people, which leads to looking up one day and realizing you've ended up with great friendships and considerable influence.

A great church is built on a group of people who are committed to God's vision, who are willing to sacrifice for that vision, and who are consistently inviting others to become a part of that vision.

This kind of church isn't perfect, but it allows people to experience and feel God when they come into the environment. Whether they're with the leader, the team, or the people, there's a clear culture that comes through because the whole church is united under the same vision.

The enemy hates these kinds of environments. He only has two moves: *lie* and *divide.*

Wherever people are using their gifts to serve one another, build the Church, and advance a Kingdom vision, you can be certain he and his minions will be working to sabotage and disrupt the progress.

And in our low moments, when we're doubting our call, the enemy comes and lies to us.

- **He tells us no one sees and no one cares.**
- **He lies about our teammates.**
- **He reminds us how tired we are and how little we're accomplishing.**

It's no wonder so many ministry leaders burn out or give up. This is what happened to Peter.

Peter was the one disciple who stepped out of the boat to follow Jesus in the storm.[12] He was the only one with the right answer when Jesus asked who He was.[13] Peter boldly promised never to deny Jesus . . . until he did. On the worst night of their lives.[14]

Understandably, he was ashamed, embarrassed, and felt defeated. He did what most of us would do. He quit. He went back to fishing—the thing he knew best before he met Jesus.

But the Good Shepherd goes looking for the sheep when they wander off.

In John 21, Jesus goes and finds Peter. Just like the first time in Luke 5, Jesus gives Peter a fishing lesson that changes his catch from "nothing" to "so many fish their nets could break."

When Peter gets back to the shore, Jesus restores him. Peter may have given up on himself, but Jesus still had full confidence in his future.

Peter denied Jesus three times, so now Jesus gives him a do-over. Jesus basically says, "Don't quit . . . It's not over . . . You're not disqualified . . . Let's try this again."

He doesn't rehash Peter's mistakes. Instead, Jesus appeals to the greatest motivator: *love*. Three times He asks, "Peter, do you love Me?" Each time Peter says a version of, "Lord, You know I do!"

And each time Jesus makes it so simple: *Feed. My. Sheep.*

Wait a minute. Peter was a fisherman. His boat just broke again from the large haul of fish. So why is Jesus talking about sheep?

Jesus isn't looking backward to what Peter had done—He's looking forward to what He called Peter to do. Peter was there the day Jesus called Himself the Good Shepherd. He just watched the Good Shepherd lay His life down for His sheep. He knew what this meant.

THREE SIMPLE WORDS CLARIFIED PETER'S WHOLE FUTURE: FEED. MY. SHEEP.

That's what it means to be called. Love people. Serve them. Help them grow. It's like He's saying, "If you really love Me, Peter . . . if you really want to prove how committed you are to Me, the way you show it is by feeding My sheep."

You've probably realized it by now, but I don't think Jesus was only speaking to Peter. I think that's what He's saying to all of us.

Do you love Me? Are you willing to answer My call to ministry? When you're disappointed, frustrated, discouraged, and you feel like quitting, come back to three simple words: Feed. My. Sheep.

It's so simple we can easily miss it. Too often, too many of us have. I'm included in that group.

What does Jesus want from us? Feed His sheep. Take care of them. Love them the way He loves them. Help them grow.

That's what it means to be called by God.

If this resonates with you, if you sense God reaffirming and reawakening this motivation, I want to invite you to think about what this means for each of us and how it changes the way we approach ministry. My prayer is that along the way, you'll hear beyond my words and instead hear the clear, loving words of the Good Shepherd.

We can't call ourselves. He's the One who calls us. And He's the One ready to adjust and confirm your calling.

KEY TAKEAWAYS

CHAPTER 1

! Every follower of Christ is created by God with a purpose and is called to a holy life.

! As ministry leaders, we have different responsibilities and positions on the team, but all of us are moving toward the same goal. Your contribution matters.

! Ministry comes with enormous pressure. No matter what role we have or where we serve, trying to be something we're not saps our strength and puts us on the fast track toward burnout.

! Today, people often think ministry means being a platform personality, an influencer, a conference speaker, or a dynamic leader. We may do some of these things, but they're not the primary goal. The Bible says, "Be a shepherd."

! A great church is built on a group of people who are committed to God's vision, who are willing to sacrifice for that vision, and who are consistently inviting others to become a part of that vision.

! When you're disappointed, frustrated, discouraged, and you feel like quitting, come back to three simple words: Feed. My. Sheep.

CHAPTER 1

Why Do We Need to Win with People?

DISCUSSION

1. How does the simplicity of "Feed. My. Sheep." shape your understanding of ministry? What would it look like in your role to "Feed. My. Sheep."?

2. How have you seen comparison negatively impact a ministry or team? Could this have been avoided? How?

3. Describe where you see yourself in relation to your ministry calling.

CHAPTER 1

Why Do We Need to Win with People?

APPLICATION

1. **Personal Reflection:** Spend 10 minutes reflecting on your call to ministry.

2. How did you receive that call from Jesus, and how did you feel when you first said "Yes"?

   A. What did you think your "Yes" would entail?

   B. How does reflecting on your initial calling impact your current perspective of ministry?

3. **Action Step:** Think of a church staff member or volunteer you can encourage this week.

   A. What's a contribution they have made recently that you can affirm?

   B. Write them a note, send a message, or thank them in person for what they do.

CHAPTER TWO

SHEPHERDS SMELL LIKE SHEEP

"Ministry would be amazing . . . if I didn't have to deal with the people!"

To be clear, those aren't my words. But I have heard some form of this phrase from people in all kinds of vocational ministry all across the country. Why do so many of us feel this way?

Because people have issues. They have all kinds of opinions and feelings. They often don't do the things we want them to and do the things we wish they wouldn't.

They live in the gap between who they aspire to be and who they actually are. They don't want to go where you're trying to lead them. They resist you the whole way. And when they get there, they say, "We did it!" This is the human experience.

I'll never forget the moment in seminary when one of my distinguished professors warned us not to get too close to the people. *Keep your distance. Don't let your guard down. Don't get your hopes up. Don't lean on them.*

Why? Because the sheep bite.

Here's the problem with this approach: If you're called to ministry, people ARE the job. What is Jesus thinking about? People. That's what He cares about. That's what He's called us to do on His behalf—take care of His people.

You can only take care of the sheep if you're close to them. Shepherding is not a remote job. You can't work from home. Shepherds want more FOR the sheep than they want FROM them.

**SHEPHERDS SMELL LIKE SHEEP.
THAT'S WHERE THEY SPEND THEIR TIME.
THAT'S WHAT THEY DO.**

We're not trying to create perfect worship services or secure flawless theology. We take care of sheep. We serve people with the love of Jesus so they can know and love Him and grow in their relationship with God.

The Church is the body of Christ and the family of God. It's people.

Jesus said He came to seek and save the lost.[1] When Jesus promised to build His Church in Matthew 16:18, He was talking about more than brick and mortar. Buildings and programs can be wonderful tools when they help us love and serve people.

Jesus was laser-focused on every brother and sister who His atoning death and victorious resurrection transferred from the kingdom of darkness to the Kingdom of eternal and glorious light.

This is the way of the Kingdom. He is the Shepherd who leaves the ninety-nine for the one lost sheep. There is more joy in heaven when one sinner repents and comes home than over ninety-nine righteous people.[2]

That's who called us. This is what He's called us to.

At this point you may be asking, "Jeff, how can you be so sure? How do we know ministry is like being a shepherd?" Great questions. Let's think about it together.

First, the term "pastor" as most of us think about it is only used in the New Testament. And every time pastor is mentioned, the Greek word used is *poimén,* which literally means "shepherd."

IN THE NEW TESTAMENT, THE TERMS *PASTOR* AND *SHEPHERD* ARE USED INTERCHANGEABLY.

Second, there's a clear pattern in Scripture of viewing leaders as shepherds. The two most iconic leaders in the Old Testament, David and Moses, were both shepherds. The two primary leaders of the New Testament, Peter and Paul, both instruct leaders to be shepherds.

Third, God Himself is described as a shepherd. David begins Psalm 23, the most well-known psalm, with this sentence: "The Lord is my shepherd."

And finally, as we've seen, Jesus identifies Himself as the fulfillment of Psalm 23, the Good Shepherd who lays down His life for the sheep.

In addition to these reasons, let's turn our attention back to Peter, who provides the most detailed explanation of how pastors have been called to serve like shepherds.

Have you ever had a well-meaning person tell you, "We should be like the early church"? If I allowed myself unfiltered sarcasm, I would say, "What a great idea! Did you come up with that on your own? I wonder if anyone has ever thought of that!" It makes me laugh. It sounds so spiritual.

But it also means they probably haven't read much of the New Testament because life in the early church was straight-up crazy-town. Some days they saw supernatural miracles only to undergo intense persecution and suffering the next. It was a non-stop roller-coaster ride.

Toward the end of his life, Peter wrote several letters to Christians scattered throughout Asia Minor who were facing tremendous suffering and persecution.

Peter lived an extraordinary life. Perhaps no other character in Scripture endured as many spectacular ups and downs as Peter.[3]

↑ When Jesus called the disciples out of the boat and into the storm, only Peter took a few steps on the water.

↓ Of course, he sank and had to be rescued.

↑ When Peter called Jesus "the Christ," Jesus said he was blessed with divine revelation straight from God.

↓ Moments later, Jesus called Peter "Satan" and told him to get out of the way.

↑ At the Last Supper, Jesus told Peter that He was praying for him that his faith would not fail.

↓ Peter had to feel encouraged by this . . . until Jesus explained the reason was that Satan had demanded to sift him like wheat.

↑ Peter confidently declared to Jesus, "I will never deny You!"

↓ Just hours later, he denied Jesus three times.

Despite Peter's shortcomings, Jesus believed in his call. He affirmed his potential despite his failures.

Not long after Jesus restored Peter on the shoreline in John 21, Peter preached on the Day of Pentecost and 3,000 people gave their lives to Christ.[4] Think about that. I think most of us miss how disruptive this would have been.

Before the early church had a venue, before they held preview services and finished their branding—one gathering and they were instantly a megachurch. They're also being dragged before the religious leaders and the Roman officials on trumped-up charges. They're beaten, threatened, and thrown in jail.

Peter and the other disciples are doing their best to take care of the people. They're sharing resources, eating together, worshipping and teaching, and were constantly devoting themselves to prayer.

But one couple, Ananias and Sapphira, sold a piece of property and lied about how much money they made . . . and they dropped dead.[5] As you would imagine, the whole church freaked out.

Then they realized they needed to restructure in order to make sure everyone (especially widows) got food each day. They prayed and selected a volunteer team to lead the food program and one of these "waiters" named Stephen was so powerful with his preaching and teaching they brought him before a religious council.

His words were so convicting and anointed that the religious leaders killed him on the spot.[6] While everyone mourned the death of Stephen, persecution broke out throughout the whole region.

All of this happened within the first few years of Peter leading this new megachurch in Jerusalem.

Bible scholars speculate Peter is likely writing the words we're about to read around thirty years later. He's coming to the end of his life. His tone has changed. He's matured, become more humble, and yet more committed than ever to the message and mission of Jesus.

Let's look at his coaching to the leaders of the church throughout the region who are responsible to care for God's people. Through the inspiration of the Holy Spirit, these are also words to us today:

1 PETER 5:2-4

> **Be shepherds of God's flock that is under your care, watching over them—not because you must, but because you are willing, as God wants you to be; not pursuing dishonest gain, but eager to serve; not lording it over those entrusted to you, but being examples to the flock. And when the Chief Shepherd appears, you will receive the crown of glory that will never fade away.**

In his paraphrase, *The Message*, Eugene Peterson puts it this way:

> I have a special concern for you church leaders. I know what it's like to be a leader, in on Christ's sufferings as well as the coming glory. Here's my concern: that you care for God's flock with all the diligence of a

> shepherd. Not because you have to, but because you want to please God. Not calculating what you can get out of it, but acting spontaneously. Not bossily telling others what to do, but tenderly showing them the way. When God, who is the best shepherd of all, comes out in the open with his rule, he'll see that you've done it right and commend you lavishly.

You can feel the deeply relational tone in Peter's words. He's not giving a lecture about factual information; he's imparting something he learned from Jesus. He learned what matters most.

Peter says, "Be shepherds of God's flock." If you lean in, you can almost *hear* the impact of Jesus' words repeated three times to Peter: "Do you love Me? Feed My sheep." Peter didn't forget. He remembered what his Master told him. And now he's reminding any of us who would aspire to follow in this calling.

We're shepherds. These are His sheep.

Peter was there when Jesus talked about the lost sheep, the lost coin, and the lost son in Luke 15. Years ago, I was preaching this passage on a weekend and an older gentleman came up to me after the service. I could tell God was speaking to him. He reached into his pocket, pulled out a picture of his adult son, gave it to me, and asked, "Pastor, would you pray for my prodigal?" I was so impacted that I told the story in the next service and by the end of the weekend I had been given so many pictures and names scribbled on pieces of paper that my pockets were full. Each person had the same request: "Will you pray for mine, pastor?"

Jesus knew what He was doing when He told that story.

Peter personally knew from experience what it feels like to be lost and then brought back home by the Good Shepherd. That's what happened on the beach around the fire.

So now he clarifies to anyone who follows this great call what it means to be a pastor.

The goal is not to preach or promote ourselves but to watch over the people—the sheep entrusted to our care by Jesus Himself. In the Kingdom of God, being a shepherd is a "get to," not a "have to."

Like so many other things, this was countercultural. We'll look at this more closely later.

Many of us relate to Peter because of his emotion, his passion, his ambition, and his flaws. He often spoke without thinking, which got him into trouble; some might say he had a foot-shaped mouth. He swung big—sometimes he crushed it and other times he went down swinging.

We would do well to listen to his words. As I read them, I

can hear the inspiration and empowerment of the Holy Spirit speaking to us:

> *Eager to serve. Not chasing dishonest gain. Not arrogant, positional, or reminding everyone how important we are. Remembering to set an example with our lives.*

Why do we do this? What's our reward for answering the call?

- **Does it come from the people?**
- **Do we expect it from our culture or our region?**
- **Do we strive to build raving fans who adore everything we do?**
- **Do we look for the approval and endorsement of our peers and influencers?**

Peter offers a different way: *When the Chief Shepherd appears . . .*

At times, ministry can feel lonely and isolating. And at other times, it's more fun and fulfilling than we could ever imagine. No matter how things are going, it helps to remember Jesus, our Chief Shepherd, is watching. He has never missed a single word, thought, or action we've made on His behalf.

One day, sooner than we realize, we will stand before Him and give an account for everything we have done in His name. My prayer for all of us is that this realization will motivate us to be guided and driven by our love for God's people on a daily basis.

Keep coming back to, "I'm doing this for you, Jesus."

It's often been said you can motivate people with a carrot or with a stick. This is a farming metaphor used to describe motivating an uncooperative animal to plow the field—either you feed them a carrot or whack them with a stick.

I read Peter's tone as "carrot, not stick." He is inspiring and comforting, not threatening or demanding. Peter is lovingly reminding us to follow the example of our Master because He is patient and forgiving. He loves us more than we realize.

In our strength, ministry is an impossible job. The task is too big. The demands are too great. If we're not careful, we can end up doing all kinds of activities that don't make the impact we desire or communicate the things that are most important.

This passage in 1 Peter 5 is a healthy reminder to get back to the main point. What does Jesus want from us more than anything? To love and serve His people.

KEY TAKEAWAYS

CHAPTER 2

! Shepherds smell like sheep because they're close to them. They spend time with them. And shepherds want more FOR the sheep than they want FROM them.

! Jesus is the Shepherd who leaves the ninety-nine for the one lost sheep. That's who called us. This is what He's called us to.

! In the New Testament, the terms *pastor* and *shepherd* are used interchangeably.

! **How do we know ministry is like being a shepherd?**

1. *The term "pastor" as most of us think about it is only used in the New Testament.*
2. *There's a clear pattern in Scripture of viewing leaders as shepherds.*
3. *God Himself is described as a shepherd.*
4. *Jesus identifies Himself as the fulfillment of Psalm 23, the Good Shepherd who lays down His life for the sheep.*

! The goal of ministry is not to preach or promote ourselves but to watch over the people—the sheep entrusted to our care by Jesus Himself.

! What does Jesus want from us more than anything? To love and serve His people.

CHAPTER 2

Shepherds Smell Like Sheep

DISCUSSION

1. "If you're called to ministry, people ARE the job." How does this statement affect your role in ministry, regardless of what that role might be?

2. What should the goal of the shepherd/pastor be? How is this goal counter-cultural?

3. What are some of the misplaced goals we sometimes have in ministry?

CHAPTER 2

Shepherds Smell
Like Sheep

APPLICATION

1. **Personal Reflection:** Spend time evaluating your current role in ministry.

   A. Have you fully embraced the fact that "people ARE the job," or have you lost sight of that focus?

   B. How can you make what you do more about the people you serve?

2. **Action Step:** Think of one or two people in your church whom you can serve this week.

   A. Write down their names.

   B. What do they need from you? How can you add value to them?

   C. Commit to serving them this week.

CHAPTER THREE

GOD'S HEART FOR PEOPLE (HIS SHEEP)

God cares about people. The call to ministry is the invitation to care about what He cares about. If we're going to fulfill God's call for our life, we need to have God's heart for people.

He doesn't see them as a nuisance or a problem. He sees them through the lens of a loving Father. He cares for them the way a shepherd cares for his sheep.

And He expects us to see them the way He sees them.

Proverbs 27:23 says, "Be sure you know the condition of your flocks, give careful attention to your herds." Another way to understand the depth of what the Hebrew language is saying here is, **"Know well the face of your flock."**

In order to know their faces well, you have to look at them. You know their temperament. You know their quirks and expressions.

You know when they're well-fed, rested, and ready for the journey. *You see them.*

This is so important to the people we lead. They need to know we see them.

Several years ago, I realized what this means at a different level. My daughter and I went to a camp and one of the relationship-building exercises they had us do was to look at each other in the face for seven minutes.

Now, this doesn't sound too difficult, but it's more uncomfortable and awkward than you might imagine. I have looked at my daughter almost every day she's been alive. But seven minutes of uninterrupted, undivided attention is a long time. It felt like forever. I love my daughter, but I wanted to be done with the exercise.

And yet, something powerful happened. I have always seen her, but looking at her that closely for that long allowed me to see her in a different way. I was able to see her insecurities, her fears, and what she was concerned about. I was able to see some things she needed that she could only receive from me, her dad.

This is our task as pastors—we have to see the people we serve. Our culture of information and comparison is making them anxious and afraid. They don't feel seen. Even when surrounded by others, they feel alone.

We have to be intentional. As leaders, we're used to setting the agenda, guiding the discussion, and getting things done. None of these help others feel seen. We have to slow down and be present. We have to set aside our agenda in order to let them know we are with them.

Nominal, obligatory Christianity has declined drastically. Most people who went to church because it was the thing to do have stopped going. But when asked what would bring them back, one answer stood out above all the others: a friend. That's all. Someone who cares. Someone who knows.[1]

Someone who sees.

The second phrase in Proverbs 27:23—"give careful attention"—can be understood as "put your hearts to them." Your hearts are connected. You are close to them. People are not a nuisance. They're not an obstacle. Caring for God's people is the primary reason He calls us to serve Him in vocational ministry.

We need His heart for His people.

Okay, so God calls us to be shepherds and the Bible calls God's people sheep. We're supposed to know them well and put our hearts to them.

So, what are sheep like? This is difficult for us because we spend time around people, but most of us have never spent any time around sheep.

Here are a few contemporary sheep facts you might find helpful:[2]

Sheep are *social animals,* so try to *prevent seclusion.*

Sheep by nature are *followers*; let them follow and *don't drive them* as you would *cattle.*

Sheep have *good memories*; these memories need to be as *positive* as possible.

Sheep like *routine,* so be patient when *introducing* something new.

When moving, gathering, or sorting sheep, the *more efficient* the operation, *the better*; wool grabbing and *rough handling* will cause *bruising.*

Sheep will *move toward* other sheep.

Sheep react *negatively* to *loud noises* and *yelling.*

Sheep tend to *move* in the *opposite direction* of the handler.

Because sheep capture a *wider frequency of sound* than humans, talk to them in a *calm, reassuring voice.* When they sense *you mean no harm*, they will *continue* with their *regular routine.*

What did you learn? What surprised you? Go back and read the list again. Underline the ones that stick out to you.

Think about how practical these insights are:

- **Don't drive them.**
- **Be positive.**
- **Be patient.**
- **Don't yell and make loud noises.**
- **No rough handling.**
- **They often move in the opposite direction of the handler and toward other sheep.**
- **They need a calm, reassuring voice.**

Does this describe the people you lead? Yeah, me too. More than anything, they need assurance, they need peace, they need comfort strong enough to overcome their deepest fears.

And if we're honest, in our most difficult moments, when we're facing an insurmountable financial need, a terrifying health diagnosis, or a relational crisis with one of our kids . . . we're sheep, too.

Admitting our need is more than identifying with our weakness. It's opening ourselves up to the Lord, our Great Shepherd.

PSALM 23

1 The Lord is my shepherd, I lack nothing.
2 He makes me lie down in green pastures,
he leads me beside quiet waters,
3 he refreshes my soul.
He guides me along the right paths
for his name's sake.
4 Even though I walk
through the darkest valley,
I will fear no evil,
for you are with me;
your rod and your staff,
they comfort me.

5 You prepare a table before me
in the presence of my enemies.
You anoint my head with oil;
my cup overflows.
6 Surely your goodness and love will follow me
all the days of my life,
and I will dwell in the house of the Lord
forever.

Psalm 23 is one of the most recognized and meaningful passages in all of Scripture. It gives us an incredible window into God's heart as our Shepherd.

It's traditionally read at funerals, but its most direct application is a picture of the abundant life God came to bring us.

These six simple verses, inspired by the Holy Spirit through a man after God's own heart, have resonated with all kinds of people in all kinds of places for thousands of years. You could say the whole psalm is contained in the first eight words.

BECAUSE THE LORD IS MY SHEPHERD, I LACK NOTHING. I AM SEEN. I AM LOVED. I AM CARED FOR. I DON'T HAVE TO BE AFRAID OF SCARCITY OR DANGER.

Dallas Willard says the Shepherd Psalm is a reminder of God's care, protection, and provision for His children. Because God is with us, we can live without fear.[3]

David wrote these words when he himself was a shepherd. Over the course of his life, he came back to these moments when he learned how to relate to God while he was out taking care of the sheep. When David boldly declares of God's goodness, His provision, and His protection, they were not speculative theories. God saved David from bears, lions, giants, King Saul, enemy armies, and even his own sinful mistakes. God provided food when he was hungry, wisdom when he was confused, peace when he was afraid, and covenant relationships when he was alone.

The first four verses require us to see ourselves as His sheep. Let's not forget: David was a boy who killed a giant and became Israel's king. But he also saw himself as a sheep.

The last two verses give us the confidence to face two of life's greatest sources of fear—our enemies and our future.

What stops shepherds? There can be a number of things, but I've noticed two of the biggest threats are offense and a fear of provision. Pastors get hurt and they worry about not having enough to take care of the sheep.

If you've felt that way, I want to speak directly to you: God has everything you need. Don't let these two obstacles stop you from what God has waiting for you if you'll keep taking steps of obedience.

Kenneth Bailey grew up in Egypt and spent decades preaching, teaching, and serving the church throughout the Middle East. He learned a great deal about shepherds and sheep from the guys who were actually out in the field.[4]

Bailey points out the unusual nature of the premise of this psalm. No sheep is ever taken to a pasture alone; it didn't make practical or financial sense. The fact that this song focuses on one sheep (us) is meant to make us feel seen and loved.

Next, Bailey explains that no one can make a sheep lie down. They only do this once they've had plenty to eat, have quenched their thirst, and are no longer threatened by wild animals or biting insects. One stray barking dog can cause an entire herd to run off without the intervention of an alert shepherd.

So, when the psalm says, "He makes me lie down in green pastures, He leads me beside quiet waters, He refreshes my soul . . ." it shows God's desire to lead us and guide us to what we need most.

The Lord guides us along the right paths. Even when we walk through the darkest valley, we do not need to be afraid because of the assistance and comfort of the rod and staff.

Bailey tells us the rod was like a mace, not a walking stick. The rod had a knob on the end to be used as a club, a blunt weapon to ward off attacks from predators and thieves. The staff was longer, useful for balance over difficult terrain, and provided the weary shepherd a place to lean.

It also allowed him to gently guide the sheep along the path.

Once the psalm transitions to verse five, David is directly addressing human concerns. A prepared table was a sign of both provision and honor, especially in the presence of an enemy. Anointing oil was poured over the head of the honored guest of the banquet.

Because the psalm speaks not only to David, but to all of God's children, we can share in His expectation that life will bring its share of enemies, challenges, and valleys.

But the psalm rises to its conclusion with faith and hope, the promise that God's goodness and love will follow us all the days of our lives.[5] Goodness and love are more than things God does—they're who He is. They're His nature more than His attributes.

Another more active way to translate "follow" is "pursue me" (NLT) or "chase me down" (MSG). This is not a passive follow where maybe you can see it and maybe you can't. David Gibson suggests the choice of the word "follow" is one of the weakest in all the psalms because this word is more commonly used to describe enemy armies pursuing each other in combat.[6]

It doesn't matter where you run or where you hide, the Good Shepherd is coming to find you, to overwhelm you with His goodness and love.

Many of the people we lead have been coached and trained to avoid seeing themselves as sheep. Sheep are weak. Sheep are dumb. Sheep are naïve, gullible followers unwilling to stand up for themselves. And so, sheep end up getting slaughtered.

In many of the places we serve and pastor, these are the prevailing cultural perceptions. Ambitious, goal-driven people don't typically see themselves as sheep.

This includes us.

And yet the Bible leans into this metaphor. When John the Baptist first sees Jesus at the beginning of His earthly ministry, he introduces Him not as the Lion of Judah but as the Lamb of God who takes away the sin of the world.[7]

We don't love and serve people as sheep to minimize them or discredit their part to play. We model for them the security, grace, and power available to those willing to humble themselves in order to receive from the Lord, their Shepherd.

KEY TAKEAWAYS

CHAPTER 3

! God doesn't see people as a nuisance or a problem. He sees them from the lens of a loving Father. He cares for them the way a shepherd cares for his sheep. And He expects us to see them the way He sees them.

! Another way to understand Proverbs 27:23: "Be sure you know the condition of your flocks, give careful attention to your herds" is to "Know well the face of your flock."

! Our task as pastors and ministry leaders is to see the people we serve.

! Caring for God's people is the primary reason He calls us to serve Him in vocational ministry. We need His heart for His people.

! If we're honest, in our most difficult moments, we're sheep, too. Admitting our need is more than identifying with our weakness. It's opening ourselves up to the Lord, our Great Shepherd.

KEY TAKEAWAYS

CHAPTER 3

! Psalm 23 is one of the most recognized and meaningful passages in all of Scripture. It gives us an incredible window into God's heart as our Shepherd.

! Because the Lord is my Shepherd, I lack nothing. I am seen. I am loved. I am cared for. I don't have to be afraid of scarcity or danger.

! It doesn't matter where you run or where you hide, the Good Shepherd is coming to find you, to overwhelm you with His goodness and love.

! We don't love and serve people as sheep to minimize them or discredit their part to play. We model for them the security, grace, and power available to those willing to humble themselves in order to receive from the Lord, their Shepherd.

CHAPTER 3

God's Heart for People
(His Sheep)

DISCUSSION

1. Do you have God's heart for people? How can you grow in this area?

2. What makes someone feel "seen"? Do you think the people you pastor, lead, or work with feel seen by you?

3. Do you see yourself as a sheep? Why is this important?

CHAPTER 3

God's Heart for People
(His Sheep)

APPLICATION

1. **Personal Reflection:** Read Psalm 23 again.

   A. How does this psalm speak to you today?

   B. What needs or concerns are you carrying that this psalm addresses?

   C. Why is it important to apply Psalm 23 to yourself before leading others?

2. **Action Step:** Look at the sheep characteristics on page 38 again.

   A. Write down a few characteristics that stand out to you.

   B. What is something you can do this week to apply these to the people you serve?

CHAPTER FOUR

JESUS, THE CHIEF SHEPHERD

Most pastors and ministry leaders I know want to grow. We want to get better. You wouldn't be reading this book if you didn't want to improve. On behalf of your team and the people you lead, I want to thank you.

You're demonstrating you have the key ingredient research has identified for genuinely improving in any industry—"a growth mindset." This means we never stop learning; we're committed to our ongoing development; we're taking responsibility and owning our part.

We're hopeful about the future, we have goals we want to achieve, and we gravitate toward people who feel the same. We go to conferences, we get coaching, and we pursue advanced degrees. Research suggests the typical pastor reads more than four times as much as the average person.

All of this is good. But it's incomplete.

At our core, the greatest catalyst for change will always be our relationship with Jesus.

- **He's the One who called us.**
- **He's the One who gives gifts, talents, and abilities.**
- **He's the One who entrusts us with purpose and destiny.**

No matter our particular role on the team, the region where we serve, or the gifts and talents we've been given, the most fruitful and fulfilling path for our future ministry will be closely connected to Jesus.

OUR BEST VERSION OF MINISTRY IS ALWAYS "WITH HIM" MORE THAN "FOR HIM."

The challenges and demands of ministry never end. Good leaders are disciplined and productive, but we need to be careful we don't grind ourselves down accomplishing targets and objectives while we miss the most important part—being with Jesus.

We're always better when we remember He's with us in everything we're doing to advance His Kingdom.

IT'S SO SIMPLE AND YET SO POWERFUL: HE DOESN'T CALL US BECAUSE HE NEEDS US; HE CALLS US BECAUSE HE WANTS US TO BE WITH HIM.

He is the Chief Shepherd and we're all His "undershepherds." It's not a word we use much, or ever. A disciple is better described as an "apprentice" than a "student." It simply means we watch what He does and then follow His example. An undershepherd is an apprentice to the shepherd.

If we want to return to the call of being a shepherd, we have to know how the Chief Shepherd does it. I want us to dive deeper into these concepts and understand how these themes appear throughout Scripture. If we're going to follow His lead, we're going to need to know how these people thought about shepherds when He began to break it down for them. There's more for us to see.

The Old Testament describes three different types of "good shepherds."

First, God Himself is described as the Good Shepherd who leads and guides His flock.[1] As we've seen, the people acknowledge God's goodness as they call themselves the sheep of His pasture.[2]

Second, David and Moses—Israel's greatest leaders—are recognized as good shepherds. This was not a figurative title or a metaphor. They were actually out in the field doing the job.[3]

Finally, the Promised One, the Messiah, will shepherd His flock in the strength of the Lord.[4] This is the Son of Man who Daniel prophesies about—who is ushered into the presence of the Ancient of Days, all people worship Him, and His Kingdom and dominion will never pass away.[5]

Jesus knew this pattern well. And of course, He understood the power and significance of Psalm 23.

The tensions surrounding Jesus' unique identity are reaching a boiling point in John 8-9. The Jewish religious leaders are growing angrier with Jesus. Therefore, when He calls Himself the Good Shepherd in John 10, He is implying they're part of a group of bad shepherds.

This notion of a bad shepherd was well-established throughout the Old Testament.

Jeremiah said, "Woe to the shepherds who scatter and destroy the sheep." Unfortunately, throughout Israel's history, selfish and prideful leaders were common. In response to their disobedience, the Lord says He will punish them and gather the flock back to their pasture Himself.[6]

This is more than shepherds who made mistakes. Both Moses and David made significant mistakes.[7] Moses had issues with his anger and David committed one of the most grievous sins in the Bible. The difference is they responded to correction. They repented.

It's interesting to note when Nathan the prophet confronted King David after his affair with Bathsheba, he used a parable of a shepherd to deliver the message in a way David could receive it.[8]

In Ezekiel 34, the Lord told Ezekiel to prophesy against the shepherds of Israel because they only took care of themselves; they ate the curds, clothed themselves with wool, and slaughtered the choice animals. They did not strengthen the weak, heal the sick, or bind up the injured like good shepherds.

Instead, they ruled harshly and brutally, so the sheep fled. They wandered over the mountains and hills and scattered over the earth. No one searched for them.

The Lord judged the bad shepherds; they were removed and no longer able to feed themselves. In their place, the Lord promised to search for the sheep, rescue them, tend to their needs, and feed them in rich pastures. He promised to bring back the lost, bind up the injured, and strengthen the weak.[9]

The pattern is clear: When the people entrusted to lead God's people are revealed as negligent or evil, He removes them and steps in Himself.

Jesus is well aware of this pattern.

He also knows how familiar the Pharisees and religious leaders were with this historic discussion. He reminds them that anyone who tries to go around the gate to get to the sheep is a thief or a robber.[10]

When the shepherd put the sheep down for the night out in the pasture or the field, he would huddle them against an enclosure and then sleep in front of them. He literally was the gate.

This is what Jesus means when He says, "*I am the gate*."[11] He's saying, "I lie down in front of the sheep. I put myself between them and danger. I take the responsibility to care for them and to protect them."

And when Jesus says, "I am the Good Shepherd," He is intentionally contrasting Himself with the bad shepherds Israel was so familiar with. In essence, He was saying, "I am the solution to the problem in Jeremiah 23 and Ezekiel 34."

WHAT DOES THE GOOD SHEPHERD DO? HE LAYS DOWN HIS LIFE FOR THE SHEEP.

Again, this is no metaphor. This is a clear prophetic picture of the culmination of Jesus' ministry.

When I was first called to ministry as a young man, I wrestled with this. I knew God was calling me, but I wondered, *Can I do it? What if I don't have what it takes? What if I'm not willing to lay everything down?*

My mom was a prayer warrior who was waiting for this moment. My dad was a pocket-protector-wearing engineer who was concerned about how I was going to pay my bills. I had to sort it out. God brought the help I needed along the way, but wrestling with your calling is part of how God grows us. He wants us dependent on Him.

Jesus says "hired hands" won't lay down their lives for the sheep. A hired hand was usually a day-worker—someone looking for work who was given temporary employment during a particularly busy season. "Hired hands" got paid at the end of the day. There was no commitment, no dedication, no dependency. Maybe you'd see them again, maybe you wouldn't.

Later on, in chapters 8 and 9, we'll get deep into team dynamics and how important they are to our ability to shepherd the flock. But while we're on this subject, I want to caution you about depending on hired hands. Don't be surprised when they act the way they do. Be careful if you build on them.

The Good Shepherd doesn't build on hired hands, and He's nothing like them:

- **The sheep listen to His voice because He calls them by name and He leads them out.**[12]
- **They follow because they know His voice—they run away from the stranger.**[13]
- **He knows the sheep and they know Him.**[14]

You know these iconic passages. But let's stop for a moment and think about this. This is what Jesus says about you. It's what He says about me: He knows us, He calls us by name, and He leads us out.

The greatest leader who ever lived.

The most influential person in human history.

The beloved Son of God.

The King of kings and Lord of lords.

The One worshipped by all people from all nations.

The One whose dominion and
Kingdom will never pass away.

The One who everything was created IN and FOR.

He is our Good Shepherd.

We can't shepherd God's people without understanding and appreciating our Good Shepherd who so lovingly cares for us.

Character is revealed in adversity. Leadership is revealed in crisis. And the quality of a shepherd is revealed when a sheep is lost.

As we've seen, Jesus repeatedly used this lost sheep language to describe preaching the gospel. When He sent the disciples out to preach for the first time, He told them He was sending them to the lost sheep of Israel.[15]

When the shepherd discovered a sheep was lost, it was immediately an urgent situation. It was a crisis. He dropped what he was doing to go find it. He realized he didn't have long. On those glorious instances when it was found, the shepherd would joyfully put the sheep on his shoulders, bring it home, and call all his friends and neighbors to celebrate.[16]

Bailey said that once a sheep knows it's lost, it tries to hide under a bush or a rock and begins quivering and bleating. From this moment on, it's a race against the predators.

If the shepherd fails to quickly locate the sheep based on its cries of distress, it will be discovered and killed by a wild animal. When the shepherd finds the sheep in time, the animal would be too traumatized to walk so it would be carried back.[17]

Bailey also points out a challenge sheep face that few other animals share—they are defenseless. Cats have teeth, claws, and natural quickness. Dogs have sharp teeth and speed. Horses can kick, bite, and run. Bears can claw, bite, and crush. Deer can run and leap with remarkable speed.[18]

Sheep have no means of attack and cannot outrun any predator. The sheep's only security is the shepherd.

We're undershepherds of Jesus. First and foremost, He shepherds us. Then He calls us to follow His example.

Do you know your sheep?

Do they know your voice?

Do you lead them out?

Do you lay down your life for them?

Do you leave the ninety-nine for the one lost sheep?

This is what He calls us to do.

KEY TAKEAWAYS

CHAPTER 4

! At our core, the greatest catalyst for change will always be our relationship with Jesus. Our best version of ministry is always "with Him" more than "for Him."

! He doesn't call us because He needs us; He calls us because He wants us to be with Him.

! Jesus is the Chief Shepherd and we're all His "under-shepherds." We watch what He does and then follow His example.

! If we want to return to the call of being a shepherd, we have to know how the Chief Shepherd does it.

! **The Old Testament describes three different types of "good shepherds."**

1. *God Himself is described as the Good Shepherd who leads and guides His flock.*
2. *David and Moses—Israel's greatest leaders—are recognized as good shepherds.*
3. *The Promised One, the Messiah, will shepherd His flock in the strength of the Lord.*

! The Good Shepherd lays down His life for the sheep.

! We can't shepherd God's people without understanding and appreciating our Good Shepherd who so lovingly cares for us.

CHAPTER 4

Jesus, the Chief Shepherd

DISCUSSION

1. "The greatest catalyst for change will always be our relationship with Jesus." How would you describe your relationship with Jesus right now?

2. What stands out to you from this chapter about the Chief Shepherd and what He does for the sheep?

3. As an undershepherd, how well are you following the example of the Chief Shepherd?

CHAPTER 4

Jesus, the Chief Shepherd

APPLICATION

1. **Personal Reflection:** How long has it been since you spent meaningful time with the Chief Shepherd?

   A. Are you allowing Him to minister to you and to meet your needs?

   B. Spend time seeking Him. Use the space below to write down anything you sense Him saying.

2. **Action Step:** Is there someone you know who is "lost" right now?

   A. Who is it?

   B. What does God want you to do to help reach this person?

CHAPTER FIVE

THE CALL TO THE SHEPHERD'S LIFE

One of the reasons Psalm 23 is among the most cherished, studied, and memorized passages of Scripture is because it applies to all of us. The promises contained in these six simple verses are available to all of God's children.

And John 10 moves us because Jesus *is* the Good Shepherd to all of His sheep. He did not speak these words just to those gathered on that day. They reach out across time and space to all of us who receive Him.

Understanding God's heart for people and loving the sheep the way He loves them will help anyone, anywhere in the world. It's a principle that always works.

It doesn't matter if you're a grandfather working in the business sector, a college student pursuing a medical degree, a mom of small children, or someone working in the hospitality industry.

When we love what God loves (people), we grow closer to Him, we become a better version of who He created us to be, and even though we'll likely face resistance, our influence and impact will expand.

A big part of growing into maturity in our relationship with Jesus is realizing He doesn't just save us; He invites us to join Him in what He's doing. Like He did with Abraham, He blesses us not merely for our benefit, but for others. Whenever He's working in us, it's always for something bigger than us.

Every follower of Christ is adopted into God's family and invited to use their unique gifts and talents to love and serve others.[1] It's not for a select few. Making disciples is not something a few paid professionals can do; it's the commission Jesus gave to all His followers. It's truly a "co-mission"—He promises to be with us always in the process, even to the ends of the earth.[2]

For most people, this is a big shift in their perspective. And yet, there is a difference for those who pursue ministry as a vocational calling.

I realize this can be confusing. In order to win with people, you have to know what game you're playing so you can follow the rules. You don't want to score points on the wrong scoreboard.

Maybe you're exploring a call to vocational ministry. Maybe you're going to school, receiving training, or serving in a volunteer capacity while you're thinking and praying about it. All of these are good things.

But the call to the shepherd's life is different than being grateful for what God's done in your life. It requires more than being excited and passionate about the momentum and growth in your church family.

Those are excellent motivations to serve and put your gifts to work in your local church. This is how God designed the body to function. Every church needs a growing army of people who share this motivation to reach its redemptive potential.

Peter qualifies his words in 1 Peter 5 as applying only to shepherds. He wasn't writing to everyone. He was writing to those who had been called and were serving in that role.

After decades of ministry and coaching and training hundreds of pastors and leaders, I can promise you ministry is not an ideal career.

The word "career" originates from the root word for "chariot"—it referred to the deadly chariot races in ancient Rome. This is not a great metaphor for laying down your life and serving others in ministry. Careers primarily focus on prestige, benefits, climbing the organizational chart, and 3-, 5-, and 10-year plans.

Ministry requires more from us than natural resources like our time or our physical and emotional energy. **Ministry tests our hearts and our motivation.** Prolonged ministry that comes only from our physical abilities eventually damages the health of our souls.

Don't get me wrong, it's also filled with incredible blessings and benefits, but I can't overstate how critical it is to be called.

Here's my best attempt to explain this process:

YOUR CALL COMES FROM GOD, BUT IT'S CONFIRMED BY THOSE HE'S PLACED YOU WITH.

We don't call ourselves. Other people don't call us. **God calls us. But this calling is confirmed by the trusted relationships He places us in.**

This is the pattern in the book of Acts. There are some similarities between moments of calling and there are some unique circumstances, but it's always connected to the relationships within the church.

In Acts 6, the disciples told the people to pray and select seven men to be given responsibility. The people prayed, presented them to the apostles, and they laid hands on them. In Acts 13, the Holy Spirit tells them to set apart Barnabas and Saul, so the leaders fasted, prayed, and placed their hands on them before sending them off. In Acts 15, the elders chose Judas (Barsabbas) and Silas to be sent. Later in Acts 15, Barnabas wanted to bring John Mark, but Paul didn't trust him, and so they parted ways over their disagreement.

And in Acts 16, Paul wanted to take a young man named Timothy with him to train for ministry. Because his father was Greek, Paul circumcised him. Thankfully, we don't see that last step as necessary.

Again, I realize this is a different paradigm than other vocations. It requires more than instruction and credentials. If you want to be a doctor, you take your entrance exams, enroll in a program, and receive the necessary training and development. Hopefully, along the way, you find mentors who develop you and help you find placement when you begin your practice.

We all would admit our historic infrastructures are being tested in today's world. The process we employ to ordain pastors or to develop ministry team members is something we should prayerfully and strategically continue to adjust and improve.

I strongly believe in the value and role of training and education, but it's not the primary ingredient. Calling comes through trusted voices and divine relationships. It emerges through the discipleship process as leaders recognize, identify, and empower people by giving them opportunities to use their gifts to serve people.

This approach is more consistent with Scripture and more natural. The Bible is more "we" than "me." It's more "one another" than one person who has a dream.

Instead of self-identifying, enrolling in years of expensive schooling, and then discovering whether or not you bear fruit in your first ministry assignment, you get immediate feedback when on a team.

Some people want to preach. Others want to lead worship. These are meaningful platform roles that help people grow. They also require gifting. The desire is not enough. And even when you have the gifting, these gifts need to be developed and stewarded through personal growth and character.

A professor can evaluate your academic capabilities, but your church family will likely have a better perspective on your process of spiritual maturity. Peter and Paul both had significant influence and tremendous understanding, but they both listened to correction and counsel and submitted to the wisdom of church leadership.

I strongly believe in the value of higher education. We started Milestone College in order to train young ministry leaders. I have multiple postgraduate degrees, including a doctorate.

Unfortunately, at each step in the process I've noticed that many of the significant textbooks and theories are created in the silo of academia instead of through practical implementation in the real world.

In Ephesians 4, Paul explains how every follower of Christ, every member of the body, should live a life worthy of their calling.

We are to be humble, gentle, and patient as we serve one another. We're to make every effort to keep unity in the Spirit because, while we all have different callings and gifts, we're all part of one body.

Then he explains that Christ gave some (many of the translations like NKJV and NASB include the word "some") to be apostles, prophets, evangelists, pastors, and teachers, to equip all the people for works of service, so the body of Christ may be built up until we reach unity and become mature.[3]

The progression he's making is critical: We're all called. We all have gifts. We're all part of one body. All the people participate in the works of service.

Some for *all*.

All the people participate, and some have unique roles, not to *do* ministry, but to *equip* the people to do the ministry.

That's a critical distinction:

THE ROLE OF THE PASTOR (SHEPHERD) IS NOT TO DO ALL THE MINISTRY. IT'S TO EQUIP THE PEOPLE TO DO MINISTRY.

Therefore, one of the best and simplest tests as to whether someone is called to vocational ministry is, "Do they equip and inspire the everyday people to serve?"

Not: "Do they put on powerful worship services?"

Not: "Are they anointed to preach/teach/prophesy/worship?"

Those expressions are valuable and necessary. But they're not the end goal. Do you like doing ministry or do you like equipping others to do ministry?

The key question is: "Do the people respond by taking steps and participating?"

Don't misunderstand—the called vocational ministry leader fruitfully participates in ministry and uses their gifts to serve as a follower of Christ. That's the first part.

Secondly, they validate their calling through their ability to inspire and equip others to join in. That's the difference.

In organizational dynamics, there's something called an "80-20 rule." The idea is, 20 percent of the people do 80 percent of the work. There are multiple factors and explanations, but it's not what God has in mind for His Church.

A few gifted people *can* do most of the work in a church. But for a church to reach its redemptive potential and to mobilize all the gifts and resources God has gathered together, it takes everyone doing their part.

This approach initially appears to be more difficult and takes longer. In most cases, that's true. But the impact is exponentially greater.

At this point, you might be thinking: *Okay, Jeff. I'm following you. They use their gifts because they're a Christian, but they demonstrate their calling through equipping others. What else do we need to know about calling?*

I'm so glad you asked. One of my passions is to help people discover their calling.

This is not exhaustive, but there are at least seven other things we need to think about regarding this subject of calling and how it impacts our lives.

First, your calling impacts your motivation. We've already mentioned this, but it's worth repeating. As Peter said, we do it willingly, not for selfish gain.[4]

The only motivation strong enough to endure all the pressures and challenges of ministry is, "I'm doing this for You, Jesus." I remind myself of this on a weekly basis. Probably more, actually. I would encourage you to do the same. It's simple, but it's so clarifying.

Second, ministry is a team sport. A ministry team is a collection of shepherds. There's a reason Jesus sent His followers out at least two-by-two.[5] The early church followed the same pattern.

One of the reasons is that your team will confirm, or "unconfirm," your calling. I realize "unconfirm" is not a word, but it's how teams work. It's immediate feedback. They either say, "That was great," or "Please stop!" Teams have a defined culture. They have distinct language, attitudes, and behavior. And the best team leaders at any level of an organization are always evaluating and improving the culture.

Third, if you're genuinely called to ministry, you're called to a lifestyle. This is not like other jobs. For starters, weekends and holidays are the highest-energy workdays.

Because we're entrusted to care for people, how we live will be evaluated. We must have a healthy relationship with money (remember Ananias and Sapphira?).[6] Like in every other vocation, people who work in ministry have moral failures. But in this role, we choose to invite the scrutiny.

Doctors take an oath following the ancient Greek physician Hippocrates who famously said, "First do no harm." Pastors are held to the standards of 1 Timothy 3:1-7, which address the leader's personal, spiritual, and family responsibilities before being entrusted with the additional responsibility of serving God's people.

This lifestyle is also more than avoiding moral failure. It's rooted in gratitude. It's the attitude, "I can't believe I get to do this," or "I'm honored just to be on the team."

It also means despite the challenges people are facing and the problems we manage, we laugh and have fun. Proverbs 17:22 says, "A cheerful heart is good medicine, but a crushed spirit dries up the bones."

Fourth, the call is to lead sheep. If we're doing this for Jesus, He sets the priorities. When Jesus looked at the people, He had compassion for them, because they were like sheep without a shepherd.[7]

Leading sheep is slow. It's often frustrating and tries our patience. If you're into rapid change, the latest trends, and constant innovation, don't work with people. You're going to get frustrated.

Some days you'll feel like you're having the same conversation over and over. But when you're called to it, you'll discover fulfillment and motivation to think of how you can become more loving and effective in those moments.

You won't resent the sheep. You'll grow to love and care for them more and more.

Fifth, your calling is shaped and developed by the people you're called to. Both people and sheep struggle with change. They find comfort in familiarity. They're deeply influenced by their surroundings.

Both "the where" and "the who" God calls you to impacts your calling.

- **What are the highest values where you live?**
- **What are the key distinctives of daily life?**
- **What are your people's greatest hopes?**
- **What are their biggest fears?**
- **What are they passionate about?**
- **Why do people move to the area, and why do they leave?**

All of these factors influence how you communicate and how you lead. Too often, pastors and ministry leaders prioritize their own preferences and perspectives instead of thinking about what the people need to hear. This hinders our ability to effectively walk out our calling. More than what we like to talk about or what they like to hear, we need to keep asking, "What is God saying to them?"

Sometimes, we pick up practices, tips, and ministry models from a different city, a different state, or even a different country and wonder why they aren't as effective. Ministry requires context because while people share fundamental human nature, all of us are shaped by our surroundings and our experiences.

You shape your context and your context shapes you.

Sixth, your calling impacts the way you process pain. There's no avoiding it. Jesus told us it was going to happen. There's no way to do this without getting hurt.

You're going to be mistreated and slandered. People are going to say things about you that aren't true and they'll hold grudges for the things you did that you apologized for. They'll let you down when you need them. You'll say and do things you'll regret. The important thing is to have a plan. We can't stuff it and we can't explode every time we get hurt.

If we don't have a plan, we won't like our response.

We need to follow our Great Shepherd's nature in Exodus 34:6-7, "compassionate and gracious, slow to anger, abounding in love and faithfulness . . . forgiving wickedness, rebellion and sin . . ."

We need to process with trusted voices. We need a pastor to give us perspective and wisdom. We don't want to dump it on our spouse or our kids.

Shepherds need a shepherd.

Finally, the call to the shepherd's life is connected to our homes. Because of this, we need to remember that everyone in our family experiences the weight of this call. It's why 1 Timothy 3 includes how we lead in our homes first.

We have grace for our kids; we're not constantly scrutinizing them. We want them to love God, His people, and His Church. At the same time, we realize we chose to abide by a higher standard, and therefore we're not free to do what we feel like doing.

You don't need a great marriage to be a doctor. But if you're going to serve people in ministry, the health of your home life impacts your ability to walk out your calling.

Our families need us to have rhythms and boundaries. Because ministry is caring for people, it's never finished. You never reach a finish line. If we're always partially pulled away, they'll begin to resent it.

The bottom line is, your kids take their cues from Mom and Dad. The way you and your spouse relate to life in ministry will affect your kids and how they see church. When you have a grateful, cheerful heart toward it, they'll follow your lead. If you're constantly grumbling and upset, it's not likely they'll be big fans of ministry life.

We also need regular and dependable moments when the members of our family know they have our complete attention.

They need us to see and value them. They need us to be present for them. I have lots of thoughts on what this means in different seasons, but here's a big one for parents of small kids: Be present each night by their bedside to talk and pray with them before they go to sleep.

This regular connection during low-conflict moments is vital to building trust and shaping their character.

In every season our kids need to know, above all else, they can always be honest. All of this builds trust, which is what our families are longing for.

Because this is an important check-point in our journey, I want to be as clear as I can. I'm not saying it's time for your final answer; I'm trying to add value through giving you a helpful grid.

THREE CLARIFYING THOUGHTS ON YOUR CALLING

1. IF YOU'RE CALLED, YOU LOVE IT.

People like to say, "Find what you love, do it every day, and you'll never work a day in your life." That's not completely true, but there's enough there to be helpful. You should love what you do. You should be passionate about it. It doesn't mean you will love every part of it, but it does mean you often feel like, *I can't believe I get to do this!*

2. IF YOU CAN DO ANYTHING ELSE, DO IT!

Ministry is not a place to be half-in, half-out. Jesus said that anyone who puts their hand to the plow and then looks back to see what else is going on is not fit for service in the Kingdom.[8] If you find yourself constantly daydreaming about being somewhere else, it's probably not going to work.

If you're daydreaming about being in a different spot on the team, that's not a great sign, either. Great team members aren't constantly doubting whether or not they're in the right spot—they're grateful to be on the team and they trust that God will put them right where He wants them.

3. THE BEST PLACE TO EXPLORE YOUR CALL IS SERVING IN YOUR LOCAL CHURCH.

This is the beauty of being a part of a church where everyone can use their gifts to serve people. You don't need a job. You don't need a title or a paycheck. There are plenty of places to volunteer, be a part of something significant, and grow in your understanding. Some of our best team members are people we started paying for what they were already doing as volunteers. This helps to make the transition smoother.

KEY TAKEAWAYS

CHAPTER 5

! Ministry tests our hearts and our motivation. It is a calling.

! Your call comes from God, but it's confirmed by those He's placed you with.

! The role of the pastor (shepherd) is not to do all the ministry. It's to equip the people to do ministry.

! **What do we need to know about calling?**

1. Your calling impacts your motivation.
2. Ministry is a team sport.
3. If you're genuinely called to ministry, you're called to a lifestyle.
4. The call is to lead sheep.
5. Your calling is shaped and developed by the people you're called to.
6. Your calling impacts the way you process pain.
7. The call to the shepherd's life is connected to our homes.

! **Three Clarifying Thoughts on Your Calling**

1. If you're called, you love it.
2. If you can do anything else, do it!
3. The best place to explore your call is serving in your local church.

CHAPTER 5

The Call to the Shepherd's Life

DISCUSSION

1. How would you describe the difference between a career and a calling? Do we sometimes (mistakenly) blend the two? Explain.

2. "The role of the pastor (shepherd) is not to do all the ministry. It's to equip the people to do ministry." How does this statement change your perspective of ministry?

3. Look back at the seven characteristics related to calling in this chapter. Which of these characteristics speaks to you or challenges you the most right now?

CHAPTER 5

The Call to the Shepherd's Life

APPLICATION

1. **Personal Reflection:** How well do you balance doing ministry with equipping others to do the work?

   A. What's something you are doing well to equip others?

   B. How do you need to grow in this area?

2. **Action Step:** Choose one of the following actions to implement this week:

   A. Identify a ministry task you can delegate to others.

   B. Identify someone you can mentor or train to take on a specific ministry role.

   C. Invite someone to shadow you during a specific task, then debrief with them on what they learned.

CHAPTER SIX

PRACTICAL WAYS YOUR CHURCH CAN WIN WITH PEOPLE

Now that we've explored this call to the shepherd's life, have you had this thought: *If we're called to be shepherds, how do we shape our church environments so the people feel seen, valued, and cared for?* Or maybe, *What do they feel when they come into our church environment? Is it what we want them to feel?*

These are questions worth pursuing.

Every home, every school, every business, and every church has a culture. You feel it when you walk in the room. You experience it in a wide variety of ways through your senses. And our culture is shaped by our values, our convictions, and our attitudes.

→ **It's not hard to recognize how a school feels about its students when you step on campus and interact with the staff.**

- **A business may say they value customer appreciation; many will ask you to post a review, but you don't find out how they really feel about you until you have a problem.**

- **You can tell the difference between a restaurant that appreciates your business and one that acts bothered when you ask about getting a table.**

- **When you come to someone's home for a meal, their body language, their tone, their words, and the level of intentional preparation communicate how they feel about your visit.**

It's unfortunate that, as pastors and church leaders, we too often forget this part.

Whether we realize it or not, when people come into our environments, what they feel answers two questions:

1. **Who are these people?**
2. **What is God like?**

And they don't ask these questions once the worship and the message begin. Whether they would verbalize it or not, this is what they're subtly wondering on their way to our weekend service.

"Church Growth" has become its own industry. There are a lot of reasons why leaders want their churches to grow—more people to preach to, a greater level of perceived success, more opportunities and resources, etc.

These reasons make ministry leaders feel better, but they don't help the sheep. They're not an indicator that we're taking good care of them.

We may have all the best intentions as we genuinely want to reach and impact our community, but as shepherds, we start with, "How are the sheep doing?"

In Mark 6, Jesus and the disciples have been in a busy stretch of ministry. He tells them to come with Him to a quiet place so they can eat and rest. They get in the boat and head for a secluded spot, but all the people follow them.

When Jesus sees the crowds of people, He is moved with compassion for them because they were like sheep without a shepherd. This wasn't typically the disciples' first reaction. The story we know as Jesus feeding the five thousand starts with the disciples telling Jesus to send away the crowds because it's getting late and the people are hungry.

Jesus tells the disciples, "You give them something to eat."[1] You get the feeling that was the last thing they wanted to hear. They had no idea that what was about to happen would be retold for thousands of years around the world. But they had to get over themselves to be a part of it.

THE FOUNDATION FOR BEING A SHEPHERD IS TO BE AWARE OF YOUR OWN WANTS AND NEEDS, AND TO SET THEM ASIDE TO CARE FOR THE SHEEP.

Often, the things that get us excited—big crowds and lots of cars in the parking lot—makes them feel anxious or frustrated. We can't solve this completely, but a great place to start is to get out of our own mentality and ask ourselves, *How would I feel if I came to church here for the first time?*

Most leaders don't start here because they're thinking about their tasks and their vision. But asking this question makes all the difference.

Since it was first published in 1936, Dale Carnegie's classic book *How to Win Friends and Influence People* has sold more than 22 million copies. One of his driving principles is this simple question: *What would I want someone to do for me right now?*[2]

This is how a shepherd thinks.

However, if you're a lead pastor or a worship leader, you naturally think about what you're going to say or do once you're on the platform. I want to encourage you to think bigger. If you wait until then, it may be too late.

I'm about to walk you through our process, and I want you to see how much of our culture is communicated long before the message begins.

What motivates a person to come to church? The most obvious and simple answer is, "They were invited."

Nothing is as compelling as a warm invitation from a trusted friend. But even that invite gains momentum from other touchpoints: social media presence, billboards, a clear and inviting presence at the physical location, yard signs, or a mailer. Together they reinforce and develop interest.

Most people, ourselves included, want to get a sense of what to expect when they go to a new place. Today that means we search online, go to the website, pull it up on our Maps app, and, whenever possible, watch a service. The average person will probably do this multiple times before they take the time on a weekend to come for a visit.

Therefore, their first impression of us will largely be formed before any personal interaction, which reinforces the importance of an excellent, authentic online presence. All churches are at different places, so the specifics of your practical strategies will vary. But whatever that strategy is, it's important you realize your customer interface communicates your heart for them.

Developing a place on your website for "Plan Your Visit" is a good investment in caring for your guests because it demonstrates thoughtfulness and reduces stress and anxiety from the unknown. When we demonstrate intention to show we care about their experience and that we want them to be comfortable, it builds trust.

Once a person or a family has made the decision to come visit, what do they expect when they come to church?

If they've never been to a church, their first thoughts are likely, *Am I the kind of person who fits in there? Will there be anyone else like me?*

If they have a church background but stopped going, the overwhelming majority of them will experience a measure of guilt. If they're unhappy with how things have been going in their lives and some of their personal choices, they will also feel some shame.

All of this happens before they even hit the parking lot.

This is why what they experience once they come on campus makes all the difference.

- **Is there clear signage?**
- **Have you prioritized parking for guests?**
- **Do you have friendly and enthusiastic people to help in the parking lot?**
- **Do you have engaging greeters warmly welcoming them?**

Carnegie said the best way to make a good first impression was simply to smile. A big, genuine smile communicates so much. Our brains are hardwired to emotionally mirror what we see. When someone smiles warmly and greets us, the natural response is to smile and greet them back.[3]

As tragic as it may sound, there are not too many places left in our world where we're greeted this way. Church should be at the top of the list. Remember, when people come to church, they're asking, "Who are these people?" and "Who is God?"

A big, enthusiastic smile along with welcoming body language and a warm greeting is more than just being nice. It communicates something completely different than a begrudging volunteer who is faking it because someone asked them to do it. It feels like the glad and sincere hearts that characterized the early church.[4]

All of this happens before they're even in the building.

The biggest reason people fail to connect in a new environment is the fear of rejection.

- *What if my kids have a bad experience?*
- *What if my spouse doesn't like it?*
- *What if I come and no one wants me there?*
- *What if I don't understand what's happening and no one explains it to me?*

All of this happens before the service starts.

Shepherds know this is how sheep feel. They realize change is hard for sheep but they find comfort in taking simple, clear steps with other sheep.

I have a heart for single moms. God gave me a genuine burden for them. I know how hard they work. I know how they worry about their kids' future. I know they struggle with feeling inadequate. And I know they're anxious about feeling judged or looked down upon when they come to church. That's not God's heart for them!

This is personal for me—my grandmother was a single mom and a young widow because my grandfather was killed in a car accident when my dad was young. She was an amazing lady. She could fix a carburetor, help with homework, bake a casserole, tend her garden, and sew a dress all at the same time.

But it was a struggle.

Because we think about single moms' experience in church, and we want them to know God sees them and cares about them, we consistently hear their stories of being completely surprised by the way they were treated. They can feel it in the environment.

That says more about Jesus and His heart than it does about us.

An efficient, high-quality kids' check-in is vital because it builds trust and allows them to interact with other people in a similar season of life who have the same desires for their children. It's also a great opportunity for thoughtful, friendly members of your first impressions team to help them through the process. When you're first starting out, many of your volunteers will fill multiple roles to make sure the people are cared for.

But think of it this way—if these needs aren't met, some people will leave before they get the chance to experience whatever else you planned for them that weekend.

A clearly marked info center helps give people a place to go who have questions or want help. A kiosk, tent, or table for guests provides a place for connection or thoughtful conveniences like water, mints, or someone to answer questions as they walk them into the service.

Your space communicates something to the people who are coming to your church. These features may sound unnecessary but they clarify who you expect to come to your services and how you want them to feel.

Award-winning restauranteur and hospitality expert Will Guidara says, "Intention means every decision, from the most obviously significant to the seemingly mundane, matters."[5] If this is true for fine dining, how much more should it be for places of worship?

We believed this before we had a permanent home. We met in a school cafetorium, a small rented church building, and a remodeled grocery store behind Taco Casa (if you didn't know, that's the House of the Taco).

We did our best to show intentionality in every facility. We all have restaurants we love, not because of the location or the décor, but because of the service and the food.

Once the service starts, whoever is leading needs to be warm, engaging, and represent the heart of the team more than their own personal expression.

Whether it's a worship leader, a host, or a pastor, they need to be careful to avoid insider language. It's important to think through the lens of someone who has never been to church. If they're experiencing everything for the first time, would they understand?

Would they know what is taking place? For example, "Are we watching people sing or are we singing together?" "Who are we singing to?" "What do these words mean?" "Why are people raising their hands?"

These are all questions that normal, thoughtful people would ask.

If your service incorporates other elements like baptisms or communion, do you clearly explain them, or do you have to be a regular attendee to understand?

Remember, the guest never stops wondering, *Do I belong here?* The more you say things they don't understand or the more everyone else seems to have it figured out, the more you message to them that they don't belong.

Most of us don't like to admit when we don't know things. We would rather anonymously fake it until we make it. The more we normalize and verbalize the reasonable questions they might be asking, the more welcomed and seen they will feel.

You may read this and assume I'm endorsing what's been called the "seeker-driven" movement. I'm not. We're driven to worship God. We are "seeker-sensitive," because we want to take good care of the sheep, but we never apologize for genuine worship, the Word of God, or inviting people to experience His presence.

And for the record, I don't believe genuine worship repels unbelievers. Psalm 40:3 says, "He put a new song in my mouth, a hymn of praise to our God. Many will see and fear the Lord and put their trust in him."

This is what makes the "Connect Card" so valuable.

We want something FOR them, more than something FROM them. We thank them as our honored guests. These are busy people who chose to spend some of their weekend with us. We don't single them out or embarrass them. We don't show up at their house.

Instead, we ask them to do us a favor so we can serve them better. In exchange for their trust with a few pieces of personal details, we commit to giving them some helpful information, praying for anything they need personally, and sharing a little gift to say thank you. All of this communicates our heart to them in a way that builds trust and increases the likelihood of developing a meaningful relationship.

The process of filling out the Connect Card is an important step for them as they come into the environment because it helps them move toward what they all want: to be seen, to be known, and to be cared for.

Once they fill out the Connect Card, all of our messaging directs them to our "Growth Track," which consists of three simple steps to help them learn more about the church, our values and mission, and how they can be a part. We also tell them it's the best way to make a big church feel small. And it's the fastest way to make friends.

If you really want to make it simple, most people who come to church want friends. It's not about simply catering to their needs, but a good shepherd evaluates how their weekend service impacts this common desire. We want them to keep taking steps because we know that in the Growth Track, they'll get our values and catch our vision. They may not realize it right away, but they want this, too. They want to understand what we do and why we do it. It helps them feel connected.

All of this happens before the message starts.

We have been thinking about and emphasizing all of the pieces of the weekend service, and we haven't brought up the message. Not because it's unimportant, but because it takes a while to get to it.

Make no mistake—when it comes to the factors determining whether or not someone ends up committing to your church, research shows nothing else comes close to the message. Eighty-seven percent of people chose it as the key ingredient when making their decision.[6]

When I first started in ministry, I prayed and asked God for a word for the people. This is certainly still part of the process, but as a shepherd, my primary thoughts are not about what I want to preach about or what I'm interested in.

As a shepherd, my conversation with God starts with, "What do the sheep need?" This requires me to get inspired even when I feel like I'm saying the same things over and over or when I'm covering the same topics again and again.

Christmas services are the greatest opportunity to reach the widest audience of people. There is not another moment in our calendar when people from so many different perspectives are open to visiting a church.

And yet, there's a very small number of Christmas-related passages in Scripture. There was this baby, born in a manger . . . you get the point. You've got a few prophecies, the wise men in Matthew, and Mary and the shepherds in Luke. Have fun. It's only the biggest weekend of the year! This requires extra energy and creativity, but that's what we've been called to.

In the same way I expect our hosts and worship leaders to communicate in a way that engages and speaks clearly to guests, I structure our messages to be clear and meaningful to people who are in church for the very first time. I want them to learn the Bible, but I also want them to feel seen and understood.

David Brooks describes the difference between what he calls "diminishers" and "illuminators." Diminishers make people feel small and unseen, while illuminators shine their curiosity toward others in a way that makes them feel seen.[7]

Through my preaching, I always try to engage the perspective of others, to anticipate their objections, and to articulate how they're feeling. Not to expose them but to invite them to consider thinking about things in a different way. Let me be clear: I believe in the power of the Word, and I always unapologetically lead with, "What does God want to say to the people?"

At the time I'm writing this book, I have personally led more than 300 membership classes in the history of our church. I stay and personally greet everyone who wants to say hello. They don't expect it. They look at me with a puzzled face. It's a small thing that communicates a lot.

I shake hands with the people in our foyer area and one of the best things a guest can say to me is some version of: "I didn't think I would relate to this, but I felt like you were talking directly to me." Hitting that target requires hard work and intentionality. If you're wondering whether or not it's working, don't just ask your team—ask the people, too!

You may be surprised by what they say. Both of their perspectives are valuable. The Bible speaks to the seeker, and it speaks to the mature believer. The tension is not as big as we sometimes make it in our minds.

Two of the things I consistently realize are that people never get tired of good stories, especially ones that makes them laugh, and people want you to be clear about telling them what you're asking them to do. Don't try to get them to do everything all at once. But if you'll give them a few clear, actionable steps, they'll do it!

A guy named Anthony and his wife, Kate, were getting baptized one weekend, and they shared their story. They both had experienced loss and therefore had not been to church in many years. But after a warm invitation, they decided to give it a try.

Anthony wasn't sure he was going to like it, but the people they met were so kind, listened to their story, and genuinely cared. He said they went on a "hot streak"—they went to church five weeks in a row and even started watching it on their phones when they had to go out of town. He said, "I never thought I'd be watching church on my phone!"

This is what we're after. More than an exchange of information, more than railing against culture or issues, we want people to experience God. When we think about practical ways to help people win through our weekend services, we want them to feel the love and presence of God.

All of the pieces are working together toward that end. Ephesians 3 says it's through the church that the manifold, or multi-faceted, wisdom of God is made known. Ephesians 4 says the church grows and builds itself up in love as each part does its work. We call it an "everyone church."

One person and their gift is not the church. But when all kinds of people use their gifts to serve and love people out of their love for Jesus, people see and feel God.

There's a meaningful quote, often attributed to Maya Angelou, that says, "People will forget what you do; they'll forget what you said. But they'll never forget how you made them feel."[8]

If you're wondering, "Jeff, that sounds good, but is it biblical?" Great question.

One of the main ways we help people feel love is hospitality—how we take care of people. Think about this: In Romans 12, verses 10 and 13 say, "Be devoted to one another in love.

Honor one another above yourselves . . . Practice hospitality."

Remember the Shepherd Psalm? Psalm 23:5: "You prepare a table for me in the presence of my enemies." That's hospitality. In the ancient world, setting your table and inviting someone in was a huge demonstration of honor. In fact, this kind of hospitality was a reflection of your relationship with God. The Lord, the Good Shepherd Himself, sets the table for us so we feel His love.

Peter is not about to get left out of this when he writes in 1 Peter 4:8-9, "Above all, love each other deeply, because love covers over a multitude of sins. Offer hospitality to one another without grumbling."

Do you want to win with people? Don't tell them you care about them, show them. Help them feel it.

And when the whole church comes together to love people . . . watch out. The impact is supernatural. The momentum is contagious.

You might be wondering, *How do we do this?* Again, because churches are at different sizes and in different seasons, this may vary.

THINK THROUGH THESE THREE LENSES

1. WEEKEND SERVICES

What is the experience like for a guest? How do we communicate to them? What do they feel when they come in our environment? Do they experience intentionality, authenticity, and hospitality? Are we communicating in clear and engaging ways? We're going to preach the Bible in context and we're going to focus on Jesus.

What you celebrate and the stories you tell communicate what you think is important. Anything you celebrate gets repeated. Are you celebrating the right things? What kinds of stories do you tell? If your stories are about current events, pop culture, or historical figures, the people may be able to relate, but they won't feel included. But when you tell stories about the everyday people in your church, they'll believe it's possible to be part of what God's doing.

2. NEXT STEPS

What do the people think you want them to do? Are you asking them to join 17 different programs and events? Or are you making it simple and clear? People want to meet your expectations, but if you ask too much of them too quickly, it makes it more difficult.

The other key is total buy-in on the part of the team. From the lead pastor to the newest volunteer, there needs to be consistent and enthusiastic messaging. This promotes trust and reinforces the idea that they can take their next step and they'll actually enjoy it.

3. EVALUATION

Whether you're a brand-new church plant or a historically-established church with multiple campuses, we all benefit from regular evaluation. The great news is, this scales for every church, every campus, and every department. Gather your staff and your volunteers and talk through what's working and what's not working.

What would it look like if you got 20% better? What would that take? What do you need to stop doing? What do you need to start doing? These conversations will not only lead to better outcomes, it will lead to greater trust, creativity, and buy-in on the team.

KEY TAKEAWAYS

CHAPTER 6

! Every home, every school, every business, and every church has a culture. And our culture is shaped by our values, our convictions, and our attitudes.

! **When people come into our environments, what they feel answers two questions:**

1. Who are these people?
2. What is God like?

! The foundation for being a shepherd is to be aware of your own wants and needs, and to set them aside to care for the sheep.

! A great place to start is to ask ourselves, *How would I feel if I came to church here for the first time?*

! More than an exchange of information, more than railing against culture or issues, we want people to experience God. When we think about practical ways to help people win through our weekend services, we want them to feel the love and presence of God.

KEY TAKEAWAYS

CHAPTER 6

One person and their gift is not the church. But when all kinds of people use their gifts to serve and love people out of their love for Jesus, people see and feel God.

Do you want to win with people? Don't tell them you care about them, show them. Help them feel it.

Think Through These Three Lenses

1. Weekend Services
2. Next Steps
3. Evaluation

CHAPTER 6

Practical Ways Your Church Can Win with People

DISCUSSION

1. Honestly assess the question: *How would I feel if I came to my church for the first time?*

2. "The foundation for being a shepherd is to be aware of your own wants and needs, and to set them aside to care for the sheep." What does this mean?

3. What are some practical ways you can help guests at your church feel welcomed, valued, and loved?

CHAPTER 6

Practical Ways Your Church Can Win with People

APPLICATION

1. **Personal Reflection:** After reading this chapter, what practical takeaways can you apply to your church to create a more welcoming environment?

2. **Action Step:**

   A. What is one specific action step you can take this week to make your church more welcoming to first-time guests?

   B. How can you personally contribute to this action step?

CHAPTER SEVEN

THE SHEPHERD'S MOST IMPORTANT CHALLENGE

Stop for a minute and think: *Who's the most difficult person to lead?*

- ***The loud, arrogant person who's always got an opinion?***
- ***The withdrawn teenager who doesn't show much emotion?***
- ***The superfan who loves everything about your church, until they get their will crossed?***

All of those can be challenging. But here's one you may not have considered—**you.** The shepherd's most important challenge is learning how to lead themselves.

Your mind can justify what your heart desires—so can mine. You can say the right things with the wrong attitude and motivation. You can do the right thing with the wrong heart.

We can make excuses for ourselves when we feel like no one understands. It's easy to feel like no one sees how hard we work and how much we truly care. We are especially vulnerable in those moments.

We're the most difficult person to lead because we are all victims to our own blind spots. We think we're better than we are. We think we're humble. We think we're kind.

But we're not the ones with the best perspective.

We are all subject to a cognitive bias known as the "fundamental attribution error." This is a scientific description of our propensity to judge other people on the basis of their actions while we judge ourselves on our intentions.

For instance, if we're in traffic and someone cuts us off, we might think they're a jerk who needs to pay attention. *In fact, for the safety of everyone involved, God needs to deal with that guy!*

But if we cut someone off, it's a simple mistake that's easily explained by our lack of sleep and all the pressure we're carrying. *God gives His servants grace and mercy in our time of need!*

We've all been there.

It's good for us to laugh at ourselves. We make mistakes. We're not perfect. But we should be growing as leaders. It honors God and it helps the sheep when we get better.

**WE BECOME BETTER PASTORS WHEN WE BECOME BETTER CHRISTIANS.
WE BECOME BETTER SHEPHERDS WHEN WE BECOME BETTER SHEEP.**

Not because it's our job, but because it's our heart's desire to love and honor God.

Remember, there's a clear pattern in Scripture—God watches the shepherds because He cares about sheep.

It may take longer than we think, but when the shepherds mistreat the sheep, sooner or later, God deals with them. No one is getting away with anything. In the end, everything done in the darkness gets dragged into the light.[1]

Everything done in secret is exposed in public. I'm not trying to threaten or scare you, but I am offering a helpful reminder that God views this responsibility as a high calling because it impacts how people love and relate to Him.

Who wouldn't want to lead attentive, thoughtful, grateful sheep? Who wouldn't sign up to serve humble sheep that grow more mature every day?

If that's what we want, that's what we need to model. Let's not just tell them; let's show them. Leaders go first.

Henry Cloud argues that leaders (in any organization) are primarily responsible for two things: 1) what we create and 2) what we allow.[2]

No one has more influence over the culture of an environment than the leader. Whether they are dialed in or disengaged, how it feels comes back to them.

If they don't like the values and the attitudes being demonstrated, they have to ask themselves, *What do I celebrate, prioritize, and model for the people? Have I been willing to challenge language or behavior I don't want?*

How important is this?

Few things are more frustrating than leading an environment you don't want to spend time in. And yet, few things are more rewarding and more likely to produce gratitude than being part of a dynamic, life-giving culture.

We don't produce that on our own, but when our hearts are right and we're doing our part, the Holy Spirit meets us and everyone on the team can feel God's presence and pleasure in the environment.

Jesus said that sheep won't follow a shepherd they don't trust.

In their excellent book *The Way of the Shepherd*, Kevin Lehman and Bill Pentak explain that this kind of leadership comes at a cost. Someone is going to end up paying the price—either the sheep or the shepherd. It costs you time, commitment, energy, and involvement. It's a lifestyle more than a set of principles. It's hard work and unrelenting.[3]

Leadership that comes from a title or position is not willing to embrace this approach. Positional leadership is fueled by insecurity and pride.

Pride whispers, "You've earned this, you deserve it, don't let anyone take it from you." Unchecked over time, pride erodes and destroys.

Anyone who serves in ministry over a span of decades will see this firsthand. The more gifted and talented you are, the more vulnerable you are to the dangers of pride.

There's a reason why Peter's standards for a shepherd in 1 Peter 5:2-4 are followed by an encouragement in verse 5 for all people to clothe themselves with humility because God opposes the proud but He gives grace to the humble.

Charles Spurgeon commented on this passage by describing pride as the sin with a thousand lives and a thousand shapes. He said there's no one who has more pride than the person who thinks he has none.[4]

This was not abstract or theoretical to Peter. He knew what it meant to put himself first, to be very concerned about who sits where, who got the credit, or who had the right answer.[5]

But now, later in life, he is a different person. This version of Peter is quick to say we all should humble ourselves under God's mighty hand. We can give Him all of our anxiety and worry because over and over again He's proven His care and His love for us.

Pride and insecurity can keep a leader trapped in their secret sin. They won't be honest because they don't want anyone to know where they really are.

If it weren't so dangerous, this desire to hide would be ridiculous because our true condition is never hidden from God.

But you can see this tendency all the way back to the very first humans who thought they could hide behind a bush or a fig leaf and prevent God from finding out what they were doing.[6] We're more like them than we realize.

THE MORE WEIGHT AND RESPONSIBILITY WE CARRY, THE MORE INFLUENCE WE STEWARD, AND THE MORE WE NEED TRUSTED VOICES IN OUR LIVES. EVERY PASTOR NEEDS A PASTOR.

I don't need to bring out the stats about how many pastors and leaders have been disqualified from ministry. It happens far too often, and each time results in pain and challenges for the sheep.

Peter wasn't the only leader in the early church who understood the importance of the shepherd/flock dynamic. In Acts 20, toward the end of his life, the apostle Paul is going to Jerusalem and the Holy Spirit has warned him he will face persecution, prison, and eventually death. He calls for the elders from the church in Ephesus and gives them a heartfelt goodbye. He deeply cares for them. He's modeling his shepherd's heart through this tearful moment. He is telling them that he's given them everything he has, but he needs them to think about this for their future.

Paul says, "Keep watch over yourselves and all the flock of which the Holy Spirit has made you overseers. Be shepherds of the church of God, which he bought with his own blood."[7]

Notice where Paul begins—watch over yourselves first and then over the flock the Holy Spirit has entrusted to your care. The order is important. In order to care for them, you have to watch your own life. It's like what they tell you during the airplane briefing—if the oxygen masks fall, put yours on first before you try to help someone else.

This is consistent with what he told Timothy: "Watch your life and doctrine closely."[8]

And it's reminiscent of his strong challenge to the Corinthians: "Examine yourselves to see whether you are in the faith; test yourselves. Do you not realize Christ Jesus is in you—unless, of course, you fail the test?"[9]

Why is it so important for shepherds to care for the flock? Yes, the sheep have been entrusted to our care, but they belong to God. He paid for them at an unimaginable price. He bought them in exchange for His own blood.

This is not meant to condemn us or fill us with guilt and shame but to inspire and remind us that the high price we pay to lead and serve is nothing compared to what He willingly gave first.

While we were sinners, Christ died for us.[10]

We love because He first loved us.[11]

We love the sheep—He *is* love.[12]

No matter how gifted we are in our natural abilities, our only hope to love and serve them the way He does is to stay close and connected to the Shepherd as sheep ourselves.

All of this drives us to humility, a posture of teachability, and a willingness to be corrected and coached. Hebrews 12:4-11 tells us He disciplines those He loves and, without correction, we're illegitimate.

One of the primary ways Proverbs differentiates between a wise man and a fool is how they respond to authority. The wise man responds to coaching with love; the fool reacts insecurely through resentment and hate.[13]

Pastoring and leading is a very difficult job. During typical or normal seasons (free from a major crisis), the hours are long, it's exhausting physically and emotionally, and it's filled with stress and pressure.

The bad news is the work is never finished and sin continues to destroy lives. The good news is, our job security remains strong. Jesus' appeal to pray and ask the Lord of the harvest to send out workers is as needed as ever.[14]

Considering all of these challenges, what do we need to do to win?

We need to regularly evaluate ourselves through a grid of 3 Cs.

FIRST, WE CONSIDER OUR *CHARACTER.*

Have the pressures of the role caused us to slip in our personal holiness? Are we employing coping mechanisms that have created a new set of problems or opened us up to addictive patterns? Is there secret sin in our lives?

How would the people who know us best evaluate the health of our relationships? Are we present with our spouse? Are we investing and growing in our relationship with our kids? What would our team say about us? Are we short-tempered, consistently unhappy, and a drain to be around, or are we adding value and inspiring others?

God's not expecting us to be perfect but He does want us to be making clear progress. He wants those who love us the most to get the best of us. He wants our growth to be evident to the people who see us each day.

If we don't feel like we're winning in this area, we become increasingly vulnerable to discouragement, quitting, moral failure, or burnout. Most leaders are more willing to try and handle it themselves instead of opening up to trusted voices because they don't want to deal with the perceived disappointment that comes from disclosing where they really are.

But trusted voices don't condemn us for struggling with temptation. Instead, they give us the ability to make the necessary adjustments to win in these vital areas before we act on desires that require a different set of consequences.

SECOND, WE REGULARLY EVALUATE OUR *COMPETENCY.*

Do we have the skills and abilities to do the job? This often changes during different seasons in the life of our church. None of us keep our assignments or responsibilities forever. Just because we like doing certain tasks and we've done them for a long time doesn't mean we're the best person for the job.

If we want our teammates to function this way, we have to go first. We have to lead with open hands and invite evaluation and feedback. All of us feel more fulfillment when we're walking in the confidence that comes from a job well done. This raises the morale and attitude of the whole team.

In Jeremiah 3, God is calling faithless Israel to come and return to Him in their hearts. When they do, He promises to send them shepherds with His own heart, who will lead them with knowledge and understanding.

In other words, He promises to send them leaders who have God's heart and character, and are good at what they do—this is how we all should aspire to lead.

FINALLY, WE DEMONSTRATE *CURIOSITY.*

We don't wait for someone else to own our personal development. A fundamental flaw in human nature is to look for someone to blame when we have unmet expectations instead of focusing on the things we can control.

What's our plan for growth? What skills and abilities are we learning? What are we doing today to get better? Are we coasting or are we leaning into the areas where we have the greatest opportunity to improve?

There's a lot of research in this area of personal development. You've probably heard of the concept of 10,000 hours—that's the estimated amount of time it takes to become great at something. But it's not just doing *anything* for 10,000 hours. Practice doesn't make perfect, it makes permanent. Our most effective growth happens in "desirable difficulty"—intentional practice right at the edge of our current ability.[15]

Leaders who win in **character**, **competency**, and **curiosity** serve the sheep well and partner with the Holy Spirit to create a life-giving, dynamic culture.

KEY TAKEAWAYS

CHAPTER 7

! We become better pastors when we become better Christians. We become better shepherds when we become better sheep.

! No one has more influence over the culture of the environment than the leader. Whether they are dialed in or disengaged, how it feels comes back to them.

! Jesus said that sheep won't follow a shepherd they don't trust.

! The more weight and responsibility we carry, and the more influence we steward, the more we need trusted voices in our lives. Every pastor needs a pastor.

! No matter how gifted we are in our natural abilities, our only hope to love and serve people the way Jesus does is to stay close and connected to the Shepherd as sheep ourselves.

! **We need to regularly evaluate ourselves through a grid of 3 Cs:**

1. We consider our CHARACTER.
2. We regularly evaluate our COMPETENCY.
3. We demonstrate CURIOSITY.

CHAPTER 7

The Shepherd's
Most Important Challenge

DISCUSSION

1. "The shepherd's most important challenge is learning to lead themselves." Do you agree with that assessment? Explain.

2. Why is pride so dangerous, especially for those in ministry?

3. Who have you given permission to correct and coach you? Why is this important?

CHAPTER 7

The Shepherd's Most Important Challenge

APPLICATION

1. **Personal Reflection:** Spend time reflecting on the areas of character, competency, and curiosity presented in this chapter.

   A. How are you doing in each area?

   B. Are there any changes you need to make?

2. **Action Step:** Select one of the 3 Cs (character, competency, and curiosity) to focus on for the next 30 days:

   A. Choose a goal for that area.

   B. Commit to taking intentional steps toward that goal every day for the next month.

CHAPTER EIGHT

WIN WITH YOUR TEAM

If you want to go fast, go alone. If you want to go far, go together.

In the world of sports, individuals focus on personal expression, statistical records, and fame. But it takes a team to win a championship.

To be clear—when we're talking about a shepherd, the picture in your head doesn't have to be one lone guy taking care of a handful of sheep. You can think bigger. Shepherds can have teams.

Ministry is a team sport—the best flocks are led by teams of shepherds. A skilled and intentional team of shepherds can care for a lot of sheep.

The great thing about the team approach is the exponential potential for growth. Jesus went all-in on the strategy that twelve committed and developed disciples could change the world. All of them had their struggles, and one of them didn't make it, but two thousand years later, His plan continues to work.

Working with pastors and church leaders is one of the greatest privileges of my life. Whenever I'm coaching, sooner or later this subject comes up. In case you're wondering, it's almost always sooner rather than later.

What are we looking for in a staff hire/new team member? How do I know when I've found a shepherd?

These are the right questions to ask. It's going to take us a minute to get there. For now, let's think about how important it is to build a great team. Look at the example Jesus set for us.

What did Jesus prioritize in His ministry? What play did He run? He went around preaching, teaching, and healing the sick. Nobody ever preached like Jesus. All the people, and even His adversaries, said He spoke as One with authority.

The Gospels record thirty-seven different miracles Jesus performed. His miracles demonstrated He was more than a good teacher; God was working in Him and through Him. They substantiated Him and made it clear He was sent by God. I've studied them for years, went to the places where they happened, and wrote a book, *Miracles*, to help people understand what they mean for us today.

But was that His focus?

Or was His preaching, teaching, and personal ministry an opportunity to model for the disciples what He wanted them to do?

WHEN WE CAREFULLY CONSIDER HIS APPROACH, WE DISCOVER JESUS' PRIMARY FOCUS WAS BUILDING AND DEVELOPING HIS TEAM THAT WOULD ADVANCE HIS MISSION THROUGH THE CHURCH ALL OVER THE WORLD.

His plan was the development of these people. Everything we do today is connected to that legacy. We have all been entrusted with an assignment that represents the historic body of Christ.

We would be wise to remember that, even for Jesus, it wasn't easy and it wasn't fast.

His teammates made a lot of mistakes. They were slow to catch on to what was happening. They jumped to the wrong conclusions. They focused on the wrong things. But He patiently kept investing in them and entrusted them with a staggering amount of responsibility.

He risked the success of His mission by giving them a critical role in the process. Remember, He told them, "The harvest is plentiful, but the workers are few. Ask the Lord of the harvest, therefore, to send out workers into his harvest field."[1]

I'm regularly praying that prayer. The only way to get from where we are to where God wants to take us is to make disciples. There's nothing more important that we're called to do. In our departments, this means we grow our teams.

If you skipped to this chapter, I don't blame you. Actually, I want to commend you for aggressively going after the help you need. I appreciate your approach.

If you've faithfully read your way to this point, I trust it has become clear that shepherding people is not overemphasizing the pastoral care of a small group of sheep.

- **It's not about laying hands on the same people over and over until they've gone bald.**
- **It's not a huddle of 8-10 people rehashing the same hurts and offenses in prayer week after week.**
- **It's not a codependent accountability group where people go round and round with the same temptation with very little progress.**

None of these are the goal.

It takes a disciple to make a disciple. And it takes a shepherd to make a shepherd. And more shepherds mean more sheep can be cared for. This is Jesus' approach.

You can find the same emphasis in Genesis 1 that you find in Matthew 25. When God entrusts things to your care, He expects you to steward it well and multiply it. When He comes to check on how things are going, He's going to make necessary adjustments.

If you're wondering what honors God and what brings Him glory, Jesus made it really clear: We glorify the Father and show ourselves to be genuine disciples when we bear much fruit.[2]

What are we looking for in a team member? What are the characteristics that make someone the kind of shepherd we want on our team? The same standard and grid we're holding ourselves to—the 3 Cs from the last chapter.

FIRST, GREAT TEAM MEMBERS HAVE *CHARACTER.*

Do they have a genuine relationship with Jesus? Remember, the only motivation that lasts in ministry is serving as a response to our love for Jesus. People who have been around church and church staff environments can easily learn the right things to say, but their attitude (especially under pressure) gives a more accurate window into their maturity.

Do they feel called not only to ministry but to *this church?* That's important. Being connected to another staff member, the momentum of the environment, or the stability of the paycheck are not the same as being committed to carrying the vision of the environment.

One of my friends helped me to think about it this way: *Do they have a heart to do ministry, or do they have a heart to connect people to the house?*

In other words, are they connecting people to themselves or are they connecting people to God's vision? There's a big difference between those two things.

All of us as team members are entrusted with influence from God because we represent what He's doing in the environment to the people. How we steward that influence is critical.

To be clear, having different values or prioritizing another philosophy of ministry is not a character issue. We're all wired differently and have different things we're passionate about. It's normal. However, integrity requires us to be honest with ourselves and others with the condition of our hearts.

Continuing to take a paycheck from an environment you're not in alignment with *is* a character issue. It may provide security in the moment, but in the long run, it's not healthy for that team member or the church.

SECOND, WINNING TEAMS HAVE *COMPETENCY.*

They put the right players in the right positions so they can run the right plays. Again, Jesus said we show ourselves to be His disciples when we bear much fruit.

Fruitfulness is not defined as vague spiritual knowledge or random religious activity. Biblical fruitfulness impacts the lives of real people. It changes how they think, how they live, their relationships, and the quality of their lives.

If you're in a grocery store, where do you find the fruit? The produce department. That's not an accident. Fruit is tangible. You can touch it. It's a resource that's produced.

Fruitful shepherds watch over healthy sheep who reproduce and expand the flock. In practical work language, they use their gifts to get things done. This provides lift for the whole team.

Genuine enthusiasm for the church is not enough to hire someone. A desire to be around church more often is not enough. Being a person the staff likes to hang out with is not a good reason, either. We can't be so spiritual we forget to ask: "Are they skilled and gifted in the requirements of the job? Are they good?"

Ideally they're good at more than just tasks; they're good with people too. They're team builders. They make things and people around them better. One of the most obvious indicators we overlook is how the people respond. *How do the people they're serving feel about them? How does the rest of the team feel? How would they respond to a transition?*

These are only partial indicators, but they do provide valuable feedback on an individual's competency.

A good shepherd has a good flock of sheep. Again, Proverbs tells us we should know the condition of our sheep—what do we see when we look in their faces? Are they anxious and afraid, or are they healthy and at peace?

THIRD, THE TEAM MEMBERS YOU WANT ARE *CURIOUS.*

They're not watching the clock or doing the bare minimum. They're not constantly thinking about ways to get away on vacation or to do something else. They have more vision for their role than you do. Leaders aren't motivated by status quo—they're thinking about where they're going.

They're also not waiting around for the right circumstances or opportunities to be developed. They own their own development. They have a plan to get better. They're initiating the conversations around personal growth, expansion, and new ideas. Not because they're dissatisfied, but because they're excited about the future.

We want our teams to look like the church Paul describes in Ephesians 4:14-16. Not infants tossed back and forth by all kinds of crazy ideas and deceitful schemes, but people who speak the truth in love to each other and grow more mature in Christ in every way.

With Jesus at the center, that kind of church grows and builds itself in love as each part does its work. That church is dynamic and powerful. That church changes its region and makes an eternal impact.

Paul told the Thessalonians they were that kind of church. They became a model for their whole region. No one had to say anything about what was happening in their church because the word had spread—everyone had heard about their faith in God and what He was doing in their midst.[3]

That's the kind of church we all want to become.

KEY TAKEAWAYS

CHAPTER 8

! If you want to go fast, go alone. If you want to go far, go together. Ministry is a team sport—the best flocks are led by teams of shepherds.

! Jesus' primary focus was building and developing His team that would advance His mission through the Church all over the world.

! The only way to get from where we are to where God wants to take us is to make disciples. There's nothing more important that we're called to do. In our departments, this means we grow our teams.

! It takes a disciple to make a disciple. And it takes a shepherd to make a shepherd. And more shepherds mean more sheep can be cared for. This is Jesus' approach.

! If you're wondering what honors God and what brings Him glory, Jesus made it really clear: We glorify the Father and show ourselves to be genuine disciples when we bear much fruit.

KEY TAKEAWAYS

CHAPTER 8

What are we looking for in a team member?

1. Great team members have CHARACTER.
2. Winning teams have COMPETENCY.
3. The team members you want are CURIOUS.

We want our teams to look like the church Paul describes in Ephesians 4:14-16. Not infants tossed back and forth by all kinds of crazy ideas and deceitful schemes, but people who speak the truth in love to each other and grow more mature in Christ in every way.

CHAPTER 8

Win with Your Team

DISCUSSION

1. "Ministry is a team sport." Why is this important to remember?

2. After reading the chapter, how would you define the three characteristics of a good teammate?

   A. Character –

   B. Competency –

   C. Curiosity –

3. Which of the three characteristics of a good teammate is most important? Why?

CHAPTER 8

Win with Your Team

APPLICATION

1. **Personal Reflection:** Think about the three characteristics of a good teammate. How well are you doing in these areas?

   A. Rate yourself for each of these characteristics on a scale of 1-10.

   B. Where are you doing well?

   C. Where do you need to grow?

2. **Action Step:** Set up a time to talk with your pastor or ministry leader this week.

   A. Share your assessment with them and ask for their honest feedback. Ask for areas where you can grow.

CHAPTER NINE

HOW TO HELP THE HERD WIN

Sheep are among the most widespread livestock animals in the world. Because they adapt quickly to nearly all geographical locations and climates, sheep farming is one of mankind's oldest professions.

Because sheep are herd animals, they prefer staying close to the safety and security of the rest of the flock. In most circumstances, this instinct is beneficial and leads to an increased measure of health and longevity.

Perhaps the most significant exception is when one of the sheep becomes sick or diseased.

Proper herd management is vital to identify and isolate the infected sheep in order to prevent the contagious spread of dangerous diseases. Respiratory viruses like pneumonia or bacterial infections like foot rot are highly contagious and spread so quickly from animal to animal that they can threaten the entire herd.

People prefer herds, too.

When the Bible says it's not good for man to be alone, it's not just talking about marriage.[1] Proverbs says that a friend loves at all times and a brother is born for adversity.[2] It also says that those who walk with the wise become wise but a companion of fools suffers harm.[3]

Teams, like herds, are contagious. That's why it's so critical we model a healthy culture, celebrate winning attitudes and behaviors, and recognize great team members.

Selfish, bad attitudes spread like disease and threaten the flock. But a generous, faith-filled, positive outlook is contagious, too. That's why it's so important to spend our time and energy working on our teams.

At this point, you're probably thinking, *Okay, now that I know what I'm looking for, where do I find them?*

I know you want this. Every church needs more great team members. You can never have too many. So lean in. I want to make sure you're paying attention. What I'm about to say is incredibly important: *This is one of the greatest vulnerabilities for the mission and culture of a church.*

In our flesh, we'll respond to this with fear and frustration. But this is a faith issue. Let's go back to the Shepherd Psalm. How does it start? "The Lord is my shepherd, I lack nothing."

Out of all the things God could have communicated to His shepherds, this is where He starts. It's still His message to us today. Peter and Paul remind us to return to the call of a shepherd. But they both have a lot to say about God's ability to provide for us.

Paul said that God will meet all of your needs according to the riches of His glory in Christ Jesus.[4]

Peter said His divine power has given us everything we need for life and godliness through our knowledge of Him who called us by His own glory and goodness.[5]

God has promised to provide what we need. That's not the issue. The question we have to face is: *Will we trust Him and lean into His provision, or will we try to make things happen on our own?*

FEAR AND FRUSTRATION WILL CAUSE YOU TO COMPROMISE YOUR VALUES. THESE FORCES HAVE LED TOO MANY LEADERS TO MAKE A DESPERATE HIRE.

They don't feel like they can wait on God's timing. They couldn't wait for the right person so they settled for "right now."

They saw red flags all over the place, but they chose to look the other way and not at the character issue, the gap in vision, or the bad attitude. They chose the WHAT over the WHO. WHAT they needed from the person was more important than WHO the person was.

You needed a team member but you ended up with a hired hand.

Jesus warned us about hired hands in John 10. They only show up for a paycheck. They don't really care about the sheep. They're not stewards. They're not invested.

When adversity comes, they run. They only see through one lens: *What's in it for me?* Everything is filtered through their interests, their selfish ambition, and their next role. They treat every role as a stepping stone.

It's basically the opposite of Philippians 2:3-4:

> Do nothing out of selfish ambition or vain conceit. Rather, in humility value others above yourselves, not looking to your own interests but each of you to the interests of the others.

The Philippians were ambitious, driven people. They were high achievers and one of the most prestigious Roman colonies. In

Roman culture, you got extra credit for stepping on people and stabbing them in the back. (Et tu, Brute?!?)[6]

Paul challenged them and told them instead to have the same attitude as Jesus—He's fully God but He humbled Himself and became a man because He didn't see equality with God as something He should grasp or take at the first opportunity. Philippians 2:5-6 says:

> Have this mind among yourselves, which is yours in Christ Jesus, who, though he was in the form of God, did not count equality with God a thing to be grasped...[7]

That's why I call hired hands "graspers." They have a dog-bowl spirit. Like a dog when it feels threatened by someone coming close to their food, when another team member gets close to what they want, they growl at them. Once you understand how they're wired, you'll be able to spot a grasper. They're always looking out for themselves.

We don't want graspers, we want growers.

GROWERS ARE THE TEAM MEMBERS WE NEED TO ACCOMPLISH GOD'S VISION. AN INTENTIONAL PROCESS IS THE KEY TO DISCOVERING AND DEVELOPING GROWERS.

Growers don't sell themselves. Growers are works in progress. I believe God is always sending us growers because it's how we develop as leaders. We have to learn to see them, get them in a process, and get them using their gifts.

There are at least five key distinctions between graspers and growers.

First, graspers start with position while growers start with heart. When someone in your hiring process is especially preoccupied with the title, the office, the box on the organizational chart, or the perceived prestige of the role, you've probably found a grasper. They wake up every day thinking, *What can other people do to help me win?*

A grower is more concerned with correctly understanding the culture, the vision, the ethos of the environment, and how it impacts the people who experience it. They're concerned with their contribution to the vision. They want to add value. They lead with, *Am I giving my best every day to help the team win?*

Second, a grasper pulls things to themselves, but a grower knows how to empower others. Graspers get concerned when they're not invited to the meeting, when they're not informed of new projects, or when something is not connected to them. They're constantly trying to insert themselves in conversations, events, or opportunities.

Growers don't start with how things affect them. Instead, they're looking for connections. Who could help? Who would benefit from being included in the opportunity? They also realize that as the flocks grow and expand, they often have less information. They don't know everything about every situation, but they choose to trust. In this situation, growers know less but they have more required of them. And yet, because they care about the people, growers say, "I got it."

Third, and perhaps most simply, graspers think "me" but growers think "we." Graspers always lead with what's in it for them. They suffer from low self-awareness. Every situation comes back to their own preferences and desires. They find a way to make every conversation about them.

Growers have thoughts and opinions, but they're mature enough to filter them through the best interest of the team. They're not worried about what's fair; they don't waste emotional energy constantly comparing themselves with others. Instead, they're quick to celebrate others and give credit away.

Fourth, graspers are opportunists while growers are servants. Graspers have a scarcity mentality. Take as much as you can as fast as you can because you may never get another chance.

Growers have an abundance mentality. They're confident God has more than enough for them. God's not looking for a reason to give them less. The opportunities in their future are unlimited because they come from an infinite God who is good in everything He does.

Finally, graspers are critical but growers speak life. Graspers think that complaining, arguing, and finding fault in others makes them appear more appealing and sympathetic. They believe they can manipulate others through the use of their words to achieve the outcomes they're desperate for.

Growers understand Proverbs 18:21: "The tongue has the power of life and death, and those who love it will eat its fruit." No one picks rotten, moldy fruit, but too often we miss the power of our words. Growers have negative emotions and low moments like everyone else, but they choose to prioritize encouragement, hope, faith, and love.

What we celebrate gets repeated. People follow our cues. Sheep respond well to words of life.

Remember, sheep are social animals so we avoid seclusion. Sheep respond negatively to loud noises and yelling. And sheep have good memories so those memories need to be as positive as possible. All of these traits require us to surround our teams of shepherds and the flocks they lead with positive, life-giving words of encouragement.

God entrusts us with growers. I like to say the local church is the most resource-rich environment on the planet. These people are in our churches. That's one of the reasons why I'm such a big advocate for the Growth Track. When I stay to the end of our membership class and shake every hand, I'm always amazed at the people who come.

Let me be clear, there are always graspers in the mix. But I'm willing to sort through the graspers to find the growers.

So, what's our process for identifying and developing team members?

It's looked different in every season of our church, but it's always been one of my most important responsibilities. I was into this from the original thirty-two people who planted the church. It's the reason we had thirty-two instead of just my wife and me!

HERE ARE THE FOUR MAIN PARTS TO THE PROCESS:

1. COMMUNICATE A CLEAR PATH FOR PEOPLE TO TAKE STEPS.

When someone comes into your environment and they get excited about the vision of the church, you need to make it simple for them to be included. If this isn't clear, you're losing the potential growers God's bringing into your environment.

You have to continually answer these questions for them:

- **How do I get involved?**

- **How do I serve?**
- **How do I identify my gifts and then put them to work?**

The people you're looking for are not sitting around looking for something to do. They're active. They're into what they're into. You have to cast a clear, compelling vision to get them on the team.

2. DEVELOP AN EMPOWERING VOLUNTEER CULTURE.

Many of our staff members started as volunteers before they made a career transition. This process gave them the opportunity to develop their skills and grow in their understanding of their calling.

The volunteer culture of any department comes from the leader of the department and the leadership of the church. This is really important.

How the leader treats the staff determines how the staff treat the volunteers. And how the staff members treat the volunteers determines how the volunteers treat the people. If you skip any of these steps, your culture won't represent your heart.

It takes more than slogans or a values page on a website to develop culture. This is how an organization ends up with aspirational values (what they want to be) instead of actual values (what they really are). If we say we value the Bible, but we don't prioritize it, communicate it, do what it says, or inspire others to read it, it's not an actual value; it's only aspirational.

Culture is modeled. And leaders have to go first.

3. TAKE THE LONG VIEW TOWARD DEVELOPMENT.

Developing a team is multi-generational. It includes everyone from the youngest in age to the oldest. Everyone has something to offer. No one can do everything, but everyone can do something. When you commit to this process it takes longer, but your bench becomes incredibly deep.

No one does ministry alone. Every small group leader should have a co-leader they're developing. This applies to every area of service—not just small groups. The best way to be developed is to develop someone else.

The result is that your activated volunteer pool isn't confined to adults. You end up with leaders from every demographic in your church.

And it also includes everyone from the youngest to the oldest in spiritual maturity.

People often come to our church, look at our team of leaders, and ask, "Where did you get these people?" I love it. I tell them, "Do you see those worship leaders? Both of them are in their thirties and have major responsibilities all throughout the organization. Blake came when he was nineteen and Kendyl first came when she was sixteen."

It's not just on the worship team. Samantha was one of the first few kids in our student ministry. After graduating high school, she went to the University of Texas, earned an MPA from the top accounting program in the nation, became a CPA, worked at Deloitte, and now runs our business office. She has the authority to tell me "no" on budget requests. And she does on a regular basis!

We're not in a hurry. We're playing the long game.

4. BE OPEN TO DIVINE ADDITIONS.
(MATURE BELIEVERS WHO COME FROM OTHER PLACES)

I'm not against posting job listings, using a search firm, or going online for specialized roles, especially in the areas that aren't immediately front-facing ministry like the business office, marketing, graphic design, or facilities.

And I think it's possible to use those methods to investigate certain hires in more traditional ministry contexts like kids ministry, small groups, or pastoral care. But I would recommend taking a slow approach because outside hires take longer to catch and model the culture.

One of our team members who was a divine addition did a great job explaining this to us at a staff meeting. She said the key to moving a plant that had already been potted was to water it, gently remove it from the pot, loosen the root, dump the remaining soil, and then place it in the new pot.

In other words, add value immediately, slowly differentiate with honor between their previous experience and their new one, be patient, allow them to adjust to reduce shock, and take care not to damage the roots of their relationship with God as you shake off older paradigms or strategies.

KEY TAKEAWAYS

CHAPTER 9

- Teams, like herds, are contagious. That's why it's so critical we model a healthy culture, celebrate winning attitudes and behaviors, and recognize great team members.
- God has promised to provide what we need. That's not the issue. The question we have to face is: *Will we trust Him and lean into His provision, or will we try to make things happen on our own?*
- Fear and frustration will cause you to compromise your values. These forces have led too many leaders to make a desperate hire.
- When hiring, we don't want graspers, we want growers.
- Growers are the team members we need to accomplish God's vision. An intentional process is the key to discovering and developing growers.

KEY TAKEAWAYS

CHAPTER 9

!

There are at least five key distinctions between graspers and growers:

1. *Graspers start with position while growers start with heart.*
2. *Graspers pull things to themselves, but growers know how to empower others.*
3. *Graspers think "me" but growers think "we."*
4. *Graspers are opportunists while growers are servants.*
5. *Graspers are critical but growers speak life.*

!

What is a potential process for identifying and developing team members?

1. *Communicate a clear path for people to take steps.*
2. *Develop an empowering volunteer culture.*
3. *Take the long road toward development.*
4. *Be open to divine additions (mature believers who come from other places).*

CHAPTER 9

How to Help the Herd Win

DISCUSSION

1. How can fear and frustration lead to compromising values when developing teams? How can church leaders avoid this trap?

2. What is the difference between a shepherd and a hired hand?

3. Which of the differences between graspers and growers, listed on pages 144-146, is the most challenging for you personally? Explain.

CHAPTER 9

How to Help the Herd Win

APPLICATION

1. **Personal Reflection:** Consider your own ministry role:

   A. Are there areas where you have focused too much on position or personal gain rather than serving and shepherding others?

   B. What changes can you make to better embrace the qualities of a "grower" in your role?

2. **Action Step:** Based on your reflection above, identify one action you can take this week to adopt a "grower" mentality.

CHAPTER TEN

PROTECTING YOUR WINNING CULTURE

If you've ever watched a UFC fight, you know the fighters make their way from the locker room to the octagon surrounded by their team while their theme song plays.

When they get to the cage, several officials check them out and give them the okay to enter and face their opponent. What happens next is so familiar, the whole crowd joins in.

Bruce Buffer steps to the middle of the octagon with a microphone and shouts, "Ittttttttt'ssssss TTTTIIIIIIIIM-MMMMMMMMEEEEEEE!!!!!!"

Ironically, most UFC fans don't realize Bruce is the younger brother of Michael Buffer who became a household name among fight fans in the '90s for his catchphrase, "Let's get ready to RRUUUMMBBBLLLEE!"

I don't know if the Buffer brothers know how to fight, but if you want to get everyone's attention that it's time for a fight, they're the guys you call.

Somebody call the Buffer brothers—*it's time to rumble.*

SHEPHERDS CARE FOR THE SHEEP AND COMFORT THE FLOCK WHEN THEY'RE AFRAID. BUT THERE ARE MOMENTS WHEN THE SHEPHERD HAS TO FIGHT TO PROTECT THE SHEEP FROM PREDATORS.

When Jesus describes the Good Shepherd in John 10, He references thieves, robbers, and wolves. He doesn't say, "If the wolves come . . ." He says when a hired hand inevitably sees the wolves coming, he runs away. But the Good Shepherd lays down His life for the sheep.

That's strong language. Can't you just yell at a wolf and wave your arms at it? Do shepherds really have to be so committed that they're ready to lay down their lives for the sheep?

If we're still not convinced, we should consider what Jesus said about "the thief." This is not a petty thief. This is more devious than shoplifting. Jesus said this thief isn't messing around. This thief has wicked and violent intentions. This thief only comes to steal, kill, and destroy.

In contrast to the thief, Jesus said, "I have come that they may have life, and have it to the full." This life Jesus is describing is the Greek word *zoe*. This life is more than existing. It's more than not dying. It speaks more to the quality of life than the quantity.

Zoe life is the best version of life. It's the life we've been created to live. It is the life that is truly life. It's the life only available from the Good Shepherd.

And the way the sheep experience this life is when the shepherd defeats the thief, the robber, the wolves, and any other predator with bad intentions for them.

If you hear one of the Buffer brothers shouting their catchphrase, the hired hands take off running. The shepherds put their mouthpiece in, head to the middle of the ring, and get to work.

This explains why David was ready to fight Goliath, even though he was the youngest brother and not enlisted in the army. King Saul asked him why he was crazy enough to fight the giant.

David said he'd been watching his father's sheep and when a lion or a bear snatched one of the sheep, he would hunt it down. Once he found the predator, he would strike it and rescue the sheep from its mouth. When the lion or the bear turned on him, he grabbed it by the hair, struck it, and killed it.[1]

Hold up. Wait a minute. Insert a BIG-EYE emoji.

David did not say he found a good sniper position with a long-range rifle and plenty of cover. He said he went close enough to these super-predators to grab their hair and kill them from striking distance.

The same God who delivered David from the paws of the lion and the bear would rescue him from the hands of the Philistine.

This is how we're supposed to care for our sheep.

Unless you're pastoring in a remote part of Alaska or Africa, you're probably not going to have lions or bears showing up to your weekend service. I have to admit, if it ever happened, I would be so excited because it would mean two of my great passions converging into one, super-bucket-list moment.

If it's not quite so literal, what is Jesus talking about? What does it mean for us today to protect the sheep from thieves, robbers, wolves, lions, and bears?

QUITE SIMPLY, IT MEANS AS LEADERS WE'RE CONSTANTLY WATCHING FOR THINGS THAT ENDANGER THE HEALTH AND THE QUALITY OF LIFE OF THE SHEEP.

In Matthew 7, Jesus is building to the end of His greatest and longest sermon, and He warns them to watch out for false teachers. They come in sheep's clothing—they intentionally look like sheep and act like sheep, but inwardly they're ferocious wolves.

Not only are they not sheep, they want to destroy the other sheep. Therefore, you can't play nice with them. You can't negotiate with them. You have to deal with them.

In Matthew 7, Jesus said we'll recognize them by their fruit—the impact they have on the lives of other people. The quickest way to recognize a false teacher is how they talk about Jesus. From the beginning of the church, all of the major heresies start with changing how we understand and relate to Jesus.

Here are a few "greatest hits" from wolves in sheep's clothing:

- **Jesus was simply a good moral teacher.**
- **Jesus never claimed to be God.**
- **Jesus didn't really die on the cross.**
- **Jesus wasn't resurrected—it's a metaphor of how we're all raised to new life.**
- **Jesus is one of many options to get to God.**
- **Jesus' death is not sufficient to redeem us from sin—we have to add our own religious works to be forgiven.**
- **Jesus and the gospel are basic—they're not "deep enough."**

If someone has posted up in your small groups ministry teaching a version of one of these ideas because they read about it in a book or saw it on YouTube, it's your responsibility to deal with it.

This doesn't surprise Jesus or make Him nervous. From the first time Jesus sent out His disciples, He told them He was sending them out like sheep among wolves, so they should be simultaneously wise and innocent.[2]

Chasing off wrong ideas and people with bad intentions was part of the early church from the beginning. The disciples weren't shocked or surprised by it.

In Acts 20, when Paul encourages the elders in Ephesus to watch over themselves and the flock God has entrusted to them as shepherds, he also tells them to keep on their guard because wolves will come in after he leaves.

In his letters to Timothy, Paul specifically warns him about false teachers at least six different times. It's how he starts his first letter to Timothy, who was responsible for the large, growing church in Ephesus. All of chapter 4 and most of chapter 6 focus on the same subject, and Paul uses some of his strongest language to describe this problem.

In 1 Timothy 4:1-2, Paul said the Spirit clearly says bad teaching comes through deceiving spirits, they're taught by demons, and the people speaking them are hypocritical liars whose consciences have been destroyed.

That's a problem.

Paul challenges Timothy to point these things out to the brothers and sisters and to have nothing to do with false teachers.[3] Paul kept receipts for these people. He wasn't playing around. In his second letter he name-checks at least six different people Timothy knew whose actions had revealed them to be dangerous and untrustworthy.

Peter had a lot to say on the subject as well. He closes his first letter with the encouragement to be alert with a sober mind because the devil prowls around like a roaring lion looking for people to devour. All of 2 Peter 2 is devoted to becoming wise to these false teachers who secretly introduce destructive heresies.

Being a shepherd today is harder in some respects because the sheep have access to more teaching than ever before. It's never been easier because of technology. You can start a podcast or a YouTube channel, throw a bunch of crazy ideas out there, build a platform, and act like you're doing ministry.

Paul's theme in his letter to the Colossians is the supremacy of Christ. He keeps bringing everything back to Jesus. He said all the treasures of wisdom and knowledge are in Jesus.[4] There's nothing deeper. He explains why this is so important in Colossians 2:4: "I tell you this so that no one may deceive you by fine-sounding arguments."

Tragically, this shows us that technology may change but human nature remains the same.

This sounds eerily reminiscent of the bad shepherds in Jeremiah and Ezekiel who benefit from the sheep without taking any responsibility for their care. I assume God will deal with these circumstances the way He always has—He steps in to care for these sheep.

Now that we've clearly established a biblical precedent in this area, let's get practical. I'm sure you're thinking, *I hear you, Jeff, but can you make this real for me?* That's where we're going next.

TWO PRIMARY MEASURES FOR PROTECTING SHEEP

1. DIRECT CONFRONTATION

Direct confrontation means we're blowing the whistle and calling a foul. We're throwing the flag, or we got a call from the replay booth and we want to take a look to see if a penalty was committed.

Someone has committed an action or promoted an attitude we don't accept.

For example, if you hear someone repeating or endorsing any of the greatest hits listed on page 161, you challenge them.

It's important to remember that when Paul is coaching Timothy on doing this very thing, he reminds him that servants of the Lord are not quarrelsome but kind to everyone. Therefore, opponents must be gently instructed in the hope God will grant them repentance so they'll come to their senses and escape the trap of the devil.[5]

For as strong as Paul's language is on this subject, he remains willing to give people the opportunity to respond. Proverbs gives several categories for misguided people: **the simple** (don't know any better), **the foolish** (ruled by desires instead of character), and **the wicked** (evil, nonresponsive, determined to cause destruction).

At the risk of oversimplification, you instruct the simple, you challenge the fool, and you drive out the wicked.

This is another benefit of the Growth Track. When I'm meeting people and shaking hands with someone after our membership class, our conversation often raises some red flags that make it clear they're in one of these three categories. As Paul directs, I'll gently instruct them to see how they respond. If they're open, humble, and coachable, it often becomes a powerful moment that bonds them to the environment. If they're willing to listen but not sure if they can do it, we'll continue the discussion.

But if they're disrespectful, disingenuous, argumentative, and disagreeable, I cut to the chase.

In those cases, I suggest they keep looking because they're not going to enjoy or feel at home in our environment. And if they try to force it, they'll end up making friends (or their spouse and kids will), which will make their eventual departure that much more difficult.

I don't do this based on personality and I don't do it unilaterally. We're a team and we appeal to each other.

2. CULTURAL CLARITY

A healthy church is built on what it's for more than what it's against. If you spend all your time talking about what you're against, you train your people to be critics. It's far more inspiring, motivating, and developmental to spend your time and energy celebrating and promoting what you're for.

This is what cultural clarity does. I tell our team all the time, "It's this, not that." What does that mean? I want them to be able to tell the difference between subtle things they might easily miss.

Because culture is far more about heart than it is about behavior. The WHY is more important than the WHAT. If you do the right thing with the wrong heart, it may look good for a while, but eventually that bill comes due.

A pastor told the story about visiting a working sheep farm in order to better understand how to lead the people in his church. When he got to the farm, he asked what the most important tool for a shepherd was. He thought for certain it would be the staff to gently retrieve a wandering sheep or the rod to beat back predators. He even considered less obvious answers like the shepherd's voice or a dog.

But the shepherd's response surprised him. It was clear and without hesitation. The most valuable tool was "the fence," because only the fence keeps them safe from wandering away.[6]

Cultural clarity is the fence that keeps the sheep safe from wandering away.

There are lots of ways to do this. We put a lot of energy into building this cultural clarity. We talk about the tuning fork. You use a tuning fork to play the right note. When a musician hears that note, everything else falls into place.

When a church recognizes their tuning fork, they realize all of the activity and energy they get pulled into has to tie back to their overall mission.

Our mission, reaching people and building lives, has to be prominent in everything we do. If we're spending a bunch of energy and resources on a project that's incapable of leading to reaching people and building lives, we stop doing it.

What are your values—the nonnegotiable, unchanging pillars you build around every day? We repeat our five values (Bible, Mission, Discipleship, Spiritual Family, and Generosity) so consistently through the Growth Track, there's no way someone gets through it without hearing them over and over.

We're constantly evaluating what we're doing through our values because we don't want there to be a gap between what we're saying and what the people experience when they come in our environment.

Years ago, I was driving down the street on the way to our building at the time and I realized in a span of three or four stoplights there were at least seven different fast food restaurants selling chicken (Chick-fil-A, Zaxbys, Chicken Express, Raising Cane's, Sonic, Burger King, and McDonald's). Some were doing better than others. The ones that succeeded knew what they were trying to do and understood what their customers wanted. They knew what kind of chicken they were serving.

In that moment, God reminded me it's similar when it comes to church. He was telling me, "Jeff, you better know what kind of chicken you're serving." There are all kinds of practical implications. Don't try to be something you're not. Stop changing your menu over and over. What are we trying to do? What have we told the people to expect? Do they know what we're asking them to do?

That's why we build a clear path for people. You can't build a family, a business, or a church without clearly defined values and processes. It's how people grow in their understanding and experience of the culture. *What are we trying to do? How do I get involved? How do I make a friend? How do I know when I'm growing? How do I use my gifts?*

We're so committed to our path that we don't make exceptions for anybody. We like to joke that if Billy Graham showed up at our church excited about what was happening, we'd tell him to get in the Growth Track!

I realize he's gone home to be with the Lord, so if he came to church there would be bigger questions than how Billy takes his next step. It's an illustration—don't email me!

A clear path is how people learn to embody and model the culture. This gives them confidence they're growing and it inspires them to invite their friends and family. It also scales, so no matter how old you are or how long you've been walking with Jesus, you can jump in and be a part.

That's one of our cultural distinctives. We tell the people as often as we can, "We're an everyone church!" You might think it sounds corny, but it shapes the way we think about ourselves.

We tell our church every Sunday, "Thank you for being a generous church!" I once had a pastor ask me, "Are they really generous or are you just saying that?" I responded, "I really believe they're generous, but I've also found that the more I tell them that, the more they're inspired to grow in that area."

It's another example of setting a goal and inspiring people to reach it instead of constantly telling them where they're falling short.

Cultural clarity and a clear path work in every generation. We don't believe the goal of kids ministry is to keep them entertained while the parents grow in their faith. We don't believe you have to wait to be great—you can be a great kid. We don't believe there is a junior Holy Spirit. We believe God hears their prayers and receives their worship as holy.

In fact, the best time to learn the Bible, to become a disciple, to learn to tithe and give generously, to discover your gifts and use them to serve others is when you're young. We believe some of our greatest shepherds are growing and being developed among our kids, and we love to give them the platform and allow them to lead.

You might be wondering, *Jeff, I thought we were talking about protecting the sheep. What does cultural clarity, a clear path, and the next generation have to do with that?*

Think about it: When the culture is clear and the path is well known, anything that deviates stands out. The people see it and think, *That's not who we are.* Not because everyone looks the same, acts the same, or has the same story, but because they're all moving in the same direction.

It's the difference between unity and uniformity. We're into unity, not uniformity. That's what it means to be an everyone church. Everyone is welcomed. Everyone is loved. Everyone has something to offer.

Unity is empowering and is infinite in its ability to include new people under a shared vision. Uniformity is constricting and it feels inauthentic and disingenuous.

Psalm 127 says that unless the Lord builds the house, the laborers build it in vain. The mission and values, the cultural clarity, the clear path . . . they all come from God. We're only stewards. He's building His Church and He promised the gates of Hell won't prevail against it.[7]

The Church is the one thing Jesus promised to build. Have you ever looked at how Psalm 127 ends? It's only five verses. Verses one and two are about how God builds. Verses three and four tell us children are a blessing from the Lord, like arrows in the hand of a warrior.

The second part of verse five, the end of this little psalm, tells us that when the opponents come to the house of the Lord, it's the children who contend with them.

According to this passage, one of the best ways to protect your environment is to train and develop the next generation. Not to placate them, but to develop them with the full mission and values of the environment, and to inspire them to use their gifts to carry the vision and advance the Kingdom.

KEY TAKEAWAYS

CHAPTER 10

Shepherds care for the sheep and comfort the flock when they're afraid. But there are moments when the shepherd has to fight to protect the sheep from predators.

Zoe life is the best version of life. It's the life only available from the Good Shepherd. And the way the sheep experience this life is when the shepherd defeats the thief, the robber, the wolves, and any other predator with bad intentions for them.

As leaders, we're constantly watching for things that endanger the health and the quality of life of the sheep.

When it comes to protecting the sheep, there are two primary measures that form our approach:

1. Direct Confrontation
2. Cultural Clarity

A healthy church is built on what it's for more than what it's against.

KEY TAKEAWAYS

CHAPTER 10

! You can't build a family, a business, or a church without clearly defined values and processes. A clear path is how people learn to embody and model the culture.

! When the culture is clear and the path is well known, anything that deviates stands out. The people see it and think, *That's not who we are.* Not because everyone looks the same, acts the same, or has the same story, but because they're all moving in the same direction.

! Psalm 127 says that unless the Lord builds the house, the laborers build it in vain. The mission and values, the cultural clarity, the clear path . . . they all come from God. We're only stewards.

! One of the best ways to protect your environment is to train and develop the next generation with the full mission and values of the environment, and inspire them to use their gifts to carry the vision and advance the Kingdom.

CHAPTER 10

Protecting Your Winning Culture

DISCUSSION

1. Have you considered protecting the sheep as a core aspect of pastoral ministry? How does this affect your understanding of your role as a shepherd?

2. Give examples of situations where direct confrontation is necessary in pastoral ministry. How do these situations differ when addressing the simple, the fool, or the wicked?

3. How would you describe your church's "cultural clarity" regarding its mission, values, and processes? Is there a clear path for members to grow spiritually and serve?

CHAPTER 10

Protecting Your Winning Culture

APPLICATION

1. **Personal Reflection:** Reflect on the concept of a "tuning fork" for cultural clarity. What is your church's tuning fork, and how can you ensure it resonates consistently?

2. **Action Step:** Develop a plan to address the following:

   A. Identify one area of your ministry where cultural clarity could be strengthened. What can you do to more closely align that area with the mission of your church?

   B. Is there anyone in your church or ministry you've avoided confronting? What specific steps will you take to address it?

CHAPTER ELEVEN

THE MULTI-DIMENSIONAL SHEPHERD

A wise shepherd with a growing flock has to know more than how to carry one traumatized sheep around its neck. They have to be experts in terrain, reading the weather, navigating long distances, the timing required to safely move the herd, and identifying water and food sources.

Shepherding is a multi-dimensional occupation. It requires a tremendous amount of strategic acumen. Caring for the flock while preparing to expand in order to meet the growing demands requires wisdom.

By its very nature, the Kingdom of God is always advancing. It's moving forward. It's growing and expanding. Jesus started with, "Follow me." That's why we're called "Followers of Christ." We're on the move. We're supposed to be growing and making progress.

In the same way, because the church is really people more than buildings, churches should be growing and becoming more mature.

This is the consistent expectation of the New Testament. Ephesians 4:15-16 explains that mature followers of Christ grow, and as they do, the church as a whole grows and builds itself up in love. That's the pattern. That's how it's supposed to work.

This is why I'm passionate about helping churches grow.

Some people say, "God's not into numbers!" What they really mean is, "I don't want to be treated like a number." I understand why they feel that way. We're shepherds. We take care of sheep. We're not business people tracking data and moving inventory . . . but one of the first five books in the Bible is called *Numbers.* And we believe good stewardship includes looking at important numbers so we can take better care of people.

I want to go back to the Church Growth Movement I referenced all the way back in the Introduction. I believe God worked in and through that movement. It wasn't perfect, but the desire to make disciples instead of "attenders" and to empower the people to do the ministry was an excellent adjustment.

Lyle Schaller was trying to solve why smaller churches struggled to embrace this model and he believed it was because pastors of small churches wanted to do all the ministry. And it's hard to shepherd this way beyond a small flock.

Schaller's recommendation was to move from being a shepherd to a "rancher." Ranchers take care of the sheep, but they have a different strategy. Instead of directly pastoring all of the sheep, ranchers pastor the shepherds who in turn take care of the sheep.[1]

Ranchers are managers—not because they don't care about the sheep, but because it's the best use of their gifts and helps the flock expand and grow bigger.

Unfortunately, the unintended consequence of this emphasis was young pastors and leaders skipped being a shepherd and tried to move directly into becoming a rancher.

This was never the plan.

YOU CAN'T BE A RANCHER IF YOU DON'T KNOW ANYTHING ABOUT SHEEP.

You teach what you know, but you reproduce who you are. You have to go first. You can't take someone where you're not willing to go.

Both shepherds and pastors get tripped up when they fail to employ the right strategies. We all know bad character in leadership hurts people. Fewer understand that bad strategy hurts people, too—it just takes longer.

Because of the way we do ministry today, most church planters have a clearly defined sense of what they think success looks like. You start with a cool brand, preview services, coaching, prefunding, and all kinds of resources.

I didn't have any of those things when we started.

When you have all of this momentum it can lead you to believe you're further along than you are. You expect to quickly grow out of being a mobile church plant and start looking for land and a permanent location. Before long, you think you'll start a campus, launch an internship program, record a podcast, host a conference, or establish a Christian school.

In your mind, this is how it goes. It's what you see other churches doing. It makes sense for you to follow the pattern of successful churches.

It's not just church planters. This same process is repeated in student ministry. The student team always wants a bigger budget—they believe if they had more elaborate events it would cause more students to come. Maybe. But without leaders to coach and disciple them, you end up back at the same place after the event.

All of our areas are at risk for the same temptations because they're led by people. And it's easy for people to think if we had more resources, a bigger budget, and better team members, we'd be much further along.

We think if we could be just like the people we see online who appear to be killing it, we would also be "successful."

But the problem is, your context is different than the church you see online. Your team is different. Your resources are different. The people you're trying to reach are different.

Please don't take this personally. I get it. I'm a visionary. I'm a futuristic maximizer. I see where things are going, so I constantly have to wrestle with the timing and the patience for the process to catch up with where I want to go.

But this isn't theory. When I'm coaching churches, this is one of the first things that come up. Not long ago, I had this same conversation several times in one day.

A pastor would tell me about the different team members they desperately needed before casually adding, "We're going to start this campus . . . in another country." Another pastor said, "Our kids team is having a difficult time. We really need to grow in that area," and then he said, "Oh, by the way we're starting a Christian school."

It doesn't surprise me anymore. I smiled and nodded.

And then I asked the follow-up question, "Does it make sense to expand when you tell me you're not stewarding what you currently have well?" Most of the time they will then say something really spiritual like, "But we feel like this is 'a God thing'!" I get it. I've been there. And I'm grateful for coaches who helped me when I was making these kinds of decisions.

Let me be clear—I'm offering my input to serve them. When they tell me God told them to do it, I'm not going to argue. But short of that type of conviction, I think we can ask some important strategic questions.

REMEMBER, WE'RE SHEPHERDS BEFORE WE'RE RANCHERS. YES, THE KINGDOM OF GOD IS EXPANDING, BUT WE'RE NOT TRYING TO GROW AT THE EXPENSE OF THE HEALTH OF THE SHEEP.

Every opportunity to gain ground is not a God opportunity. If expansion causes us to yell at the sheep, to drive them like cattle, or to handle them roughly, we're doing it wrong. Good ranchers train shepherds to give the sheep time to adjust to changes because they understand sheep.

As we clearly communicate to the sheep as trusted voices, the majority will calmly go where we ask them to. When they get there, they will adjust and learn to enjoy it more than their previous pasture. Here's the other key: The new sheep will see how calm and healthy the rest of the flock is, and they will follow their example.

People follow the same pattern. You can say whatever you want from the platform, in your video announcements during service, and on your website and social media. But your guests will take their cues on the health of your church by the attitude, countenance, and well-being of the people in your church.

It's how the process works. It's how we help them grow and stay healthy.

THREE THINGS TO CONSIDER ABOUT EXPANSION

1. DO EVERYTHING YOU CAN TO USE WISDOM WHEN YOU'RE EXPANDING.

In 1 Corinthians 3:10, Paul told the Corinthians that by the grace of God, he laid a foundation as a wise master builder. I don't have to tell you that Paul was not a normal guy. His threshold for challenges and adversity, and his standards and expectations, were fairly high.

But he didn't build at his pace or preference because he knew others were going to have to build on what he started. He challenges each of us to build with care.

As leaders, we have to be wise in how we build. We don't charge ahead and tax the team beyond what they're able to handle. We also don't get so risk-averse that the team is never stretched beyond their routine or comfort level.

In our flesh, human nature seeks out equilibrium—safety, comfort, and the avoidance of risk. Sheep want to find green grass by quiet waters and stay there forever. But that's not how life works.

A big part of wisdom is asking for help. Great leaders are learners. They're curious. They don't wait for someone with insight to come to them—they seek them out. Find someone who's been where you're trying to go.

- **Ask them what they learned.**
- **Ask them what they would do in your situation.**
- **Ask them what they see that you can't see.**

Asking for help doesn't mean you only listen when you get the answer you want. Wise people are hard to offend and they receive coaching as love, not as personal rejection.

Another aspect of wisdom is evaluating how things are going and appropriately adjusting your strategy. Not everything we try is going to work. We don't pull the rip cord quickly, but we're also not afraid to tweak things to see if they get better.

Jesus said wisdom is vindicated by her deeds.[2] In other words, we all make guesses and try things but we find out whether we were right or wrong based on how things work out.

Wise builders are hungry to learn and get better. Their ceiling becomes the floor. In other words, they're not one-hit wonders.

Their highest accomplishment becomes the starting place the next time they start a new project.

If you're the lead pastor or the head of your department, you need to constantly evaluate how far out in front of your team you are. I've noticed a tendency in leaders to move forward as fast as possible.

After you experience a little success, you may think you can enjoy yourself. You take some extra trips. You come into the office less. You communicate with your team less. You tell yourself, *I've earned this level of freedom.*

Be careful—a rancher who's never around loses the confidence of the shepherds.

When you don't come into the office, when you're constantly working on side projects or hobbies, when the team doesn't know where you're at or what you're doing, they start to drift. It's much better to let the team push you. When they suggest you take some time, when they encourage you to pursue a side project, when they communicate, "We got this. You're good," it's a much healthier approach.

2. IF YOU WANT TO GET BIGGER, GET BETTER.

A healthy flock is a growing flock. Healthy sheep trust the voice of the shepherd and follow where they lead. Growth and getting bigger are absolutely built into the recipe of how God wants us to live.

At the same time, we're not trying to get bigger so we can be the biggest church or feel more successful. We're not competing with other churches or pastors. Nobody else has to lose for us to win. Our race is not against other leaders or churches—our race is against our own potential.

The whole issue comes down to this: *How well did we steward and multiply what God entrusted to us?*

I never focused on building a big church. I focused on building big people. The truth is, when we're consumed with getting bigger, we're probably too preoccupied with ourselves and how people see us.

When we don't make it about us and we think about serving and adding value to other people, we look up one day and are surprised to see how well the people we've built are doing. They're excited about Jesus. They're becoming better spouses, parents, friends, and leaders. Everywhere they go they're making an impact. Coworkers, family members, and neighbors have started taking steps.

This is why the book of Colossians is in the Bible.

Paul was directed to go reach a group of people in a vision from God. He encounters resistance, but God helps him along the way and he starts reaching people in the city of Ephesus. He wasn't thinking about Colossae. It wasn't on his radar.

But one of the people who got saved in Ephesus was a guy named Epaphras. He was so impacted by what Jesus did in his life, he walked the seven days back to his hometown of Colossae and told his friends and family about this Jesus he met.

They all got saved and told their friends. Epaphras became their pastor and an amazing church was born because of what God was doing in Ephesus. We know this story because Paul's letter to these new Christians is the book of Colossians in our Bible.

Expansion happens organically out of being faithful with what God has entrusted to you.

Before Chick-fil-A took over the world, one of the key moments in their expansion was the first time they faced direct competition from another franchise. The team members wanted to dominate the competition and suggested they should quickly expand and get bigger to ensure their success.

Their founder, Truett Cathy, explained that was the wrong way to think about it. Bigger or smaller wasn't the issue. The goal was to get better at what they were doing. He said, "If we get better, the people will demand we get bigger."

This story has become a big part of their culture. Their strategy has not been to expand as fast as possible. It's also why you probably haven't seen one of their stores close down due to nobody wanting to eat their chicken.

Are you focused on getting *bigger?* Or getting *better?*

The great news is you don't need any outside resources to get better. You do, however, have to make some hard choices. You must raise your standards, improve your disciplines, and invite more feedback. You pay the price.

But that's how we grow . . . and none of us ever graduate from God's desire for us to get better. Paul told Timothy to be diligent to get better, to give himself wholly to the process, so that *everyone* could see his progress.[3]

3. WHEN YOU BUILD SOMETHING, YOU'RE ABLE TO BLESS OTHERS.

One of my favorite things about pastors and leaders is most of them really do love people. They care about them. They want to bless them. They want to help the people in their community, their region, and the whole world. When they hear about a need, their first thought is, *We've got to help!*

This is why they find it hard to say no to opportunities to expand. They care about sheep. That's a good thing. But you have to remember not every vision is your vision. You're not called everywhere. You're not responsible for what you haven't been called to.

This is so important.

God is not driven by need. Let me say it this way: God does not need you and He doesn't need me. He's God all by Himself. He was sovereign long before you and I were born, and He'll still be in control long after we're gone. Yes, He loves us and invites us into His mission. He expects us to be fruitful and multiply. And what we do matters.

But it's so important that we keep this perspective—we give everything we have to offer and continue to get better, but our confidence is not in us and our ability to meet every need.

Remember, Psalm 127:1 says unless the Lord builds the house, the builders labor in vain.

Jesus told Peter, "I'll build My Church."[4] He told Peter, "You feed My sheep."[5] We do our part because we know Jesus always does His part.

When we're young we start with, "Let's change the world!" That's a great desire. But if we really want to change the world, we start by changing OUR world. Jesus didn't immediately send the disciples to the ends of the earth to preach the gospel. He said to wait in the city for the power, then go to Jerusalem (where they already were), Judea, Samaria (surrounding regions), and the ends of the earth (once you've done all the others).[6]

Let me make this really practical. Scale it to your context at whatever level is appropriate. The pattern is simple:

- **If you want an intern or a team member who reports to you, make a disciple.**
- **If you want to lead a department, lead a direct report.**
- **If you want to lead a campus, lead multiple teams or departments.**
- **If you want to lead multiple campuses, lead your church and staff well.**

Responding to new opportunities always builds on top of faithfully stewarding what we're currently responsible for.

At the end of the day, if we take good care of the sheep, they reproduce and multiply. The same is true of our teams. It's our responsibility to lead them well. Even when we're managing the ranch, we honor and consider the voices of the shepherds. We remember what it's like to be in their seat.

When we build our strategies considering multiple dimensions, we honor and serve the whole flock. That's why we evaluate and adjust, we don't move too fast, we lean on wisdom, we get better instead of bigger, and we focus on what we're building.

KEY TAKEAWAYS

CHAPTER 11

! Shepherding is a multi-dimensional occupation. It requires a tremendous amount of strategic acumen. Caring for the flock while preparing to expand in order to meet the growing demands requires wisdom.

! You can't be a rancher if you don't know anything about sheep.

! We're shepherds before we're ranchers. Yes, the Kingdom of God is expanding, but we're not trying to grow at the expense of the health of the sheep.

! **How do we know when to expand our influence and start new things?**

1. Do everything you can to use wisdom when you're expanding.
2. If you want to get *BIGGER*, get *BETTER*.
3. When you build something, you're able to bless others.

! Responding to new opportunities always builds on top of faithfully stewarding what we're currently responsible for.

CHAPTER 11

The Multi-Dimensional Shepherd

DISCUSSION

1. "Every opportunity to gain ground is not a God opportunity." Have you considered this thought before? Do you agree or disagree? Explain.

2. How can we balance the desire to expand our ministry with the responsibility of stewarding the people and the work God has already entrusted to us?

3. How can the concept of being a shepherd before becoming a rancher change how we pastor people?

CHAPTER 11

The Multi-Dimensional Shepherd

APPLICATION

1. **Personal Reflection:** Honestly assess your motivation in ministry:

    A. Is your goal to be a rancher or a shepherd?

    B. Are you focused on getting bigger or getting better?

2. **Action Step:** Assess areas of your leadership or ministry where you need to "get better."

    A. Identify two or three areas where you can improve.

    B. Ask for feedback from your team and from trusted mentors.

    C. Implement one specific change to grow in these areas this week.

CHAPTER TWELVE

WIN TODAY, WIN TOMORROW

Words may inspire, but only action creates change.

Simon Sinek

By this point, I hope you can hear my heart. We're coming to the end of this part of our journey. My prayer is that you've been inspired to grow in your relationship with Jesus and to love and honor Him through the way you love people.

YOU CAN WIN WITH PEOPLE. YOUR WHOLE CHURCH CAN. YOU CAN COME BACK TO THE CALL JESUS ENTRUSTED TO HIS FIRST FOLLOWERS: THE CALL TO SHEPHERD PEOPLE.

You don't have to wait. You can do more than think about it and talk about it. You can live this way. And you can start today.

I believe when we start living this way, we can win today, *and* we can win tomorrow. It doesn't mean we won't have setbacks. But it does mean we'll see consistent and sustainable progress.

Let's say you're inspired. Let's say God has spoken to you through our journey together. You see this pattern in His Word. You're ready to make changes, but you're not sure where to start. It's okay. You're in the right place to start winning.

Or maybe you've been meeting with your team or your department and you've been going through each chapter together. In that situation, you may have gone through the discussion questions and the application sections and begun to practically make changes. If that's you, give each other a high five or a fist bump because you're already winning.

It's not a competition. I believe anyone who has made it to this point and is asking these questions, even if you've simply been studying this on your own, is already growing. Right now, as you read these words, God is helping you become a better version of who He created you to be.

And if you went on the journey with your team, your department, your campus, or your church team, God is going to enlarge you and expand your ability to take care of more sheep.

That's worth celebrating.

So, as we come to the end of this portion of the journey, the question becomes:

WHAT DO I DO NOW?

1. START WITH YOU.

How are you doing with Jesus? Before we get to anything else, the most important thing is also the simplest. You're a sheep. Jesus is your Shepherd.

We love because HE first loved us.[1] He doesn't need us; He wants us. And it's better to be wanted than needed. He doesn't love us for what we can do for Him; He loves us for who He made us to be. We don't earn His love. We *can't* earn His love. While we were sinners, Christ died for us.[2]

Before we can love others, we must receive His love. This is especially true for those of us who've been doing this for a long time. Going through the motions, doing ministry on auto-pilot, is a scary place to be.

BEFORE WE USE OUR GIFTS TO SERVE OTHERS, BEFORE WE RESPOND TO HIS CALLING, BEFORE WE CAN MINISTER TO ANYONE ELSE, HE MINISTERS TO US.

Remember Psalm 23—because He's our Shepherd, we lack nothing. He takes such good care of us that we can lie down in green pastures by quiet waters because we're not anxious or worried about having our needs met. He restores our souls. We don't have to be afraid even when it's dark and death is all around us because His rod and staff keep us safe.

Remember Proverbs 27:23—Jesus knows what's going on with every sheep in His flock. What does He see when He looks at you? This is not *what* He does; it's not a task on His to-do list. It's *who* He is. He's the Shepherd of our souls.

2. COME BACK TO THE ISSUE OF CALLING.

Maybe you've been exploring your call. Maybe you're still investigating. If you're in this place, what has God shown you? How has your understanding of calling changed through this journey? How does this call to the life of a shepherd differ from what you initially thought about calling?

What we've found is that the call of a shepherd is to love, serve, and build people. If you study great athletes or business leaders, they don't just love the scoreboard or the outcomes. They love the process. They're into getting one percent better every day.

They don't just love what the work produces—they love the work. In many ways, the work itself is the reward. We need to be able to say the same.

What's our work? It's the opportunity to give our lives to be part of what God is doing in the earth. We honor God when we use our gifts to serve people. The people are blessed and grow in their relationship with God and we find fulfillment and significance as we live out our purpose and calling.

What's better than that?

3. LET'S TALK FAMILY.

If you've settled the issue of your calling, your home is the first place you demonstrate whether you're walking in the shepherd's call. According to 1 Timothy 3:1-7 and Titus 1:6-9, family comes first. Timothy uses the word "overseer" while Titus specifically addresses "elder," but the concept points to the larger pattern of Scripture that we mentioned from Genesis 1 and Matthew 25—be faithful with what you've been given.

Both passages describe faithfully managing your family responsibilities and relationships as a prerequisite qualifying you for ministry. Both descriptions view healthy family dynamics as an important foundation to love and serve people outside of the home.

Between the wise coaching of my pastors, the input of my first-generation Christian parents, and the convictions Brandy and I firmly hold ourselves to, we determined not to sacrifice our kids or our family on the altar of ministry success.

I realize this is a really painful subject. I don't pretend to have all the answers. There's no pain like kid pain. I've preached at a lot of men's conferences to tough, stoic, non-responsive guys. The one thing that gets them emotional and desperate enough for public prayer is a struggling adult kid.

That's why we have to talk about this. It comes at a cost. It's what we really care about. The stakes are so high. But I believe we have to be willing to engage this subject because it's so critical.

My kids aren't perfect (we certainly aren't either), and our family isn't perfect, but by the grace of God, we all love Jesus, each other, and the Church, more than ever. We're making progress. We're growing.

Ministry is holistic. We don't get to use our spiritual gifts or our level of biblical insight to validate our professional ability. They get to tell us how healthy we are and whether we're growing.

I'm giving you permission to spend extra attention and energy on this area of your life. Perhaps God's already been speaking to you about this and you just needed someone to tell you to listen. Let me be that person. There's no better investment you can make.

Maybe you don't have kids. Maybe you're not married yet. This doesn't mean this part of your life is unimportant. If you're a college student or a young adult, this is one of the best ways to prepare yourself for marriage.

Do you know how to cultivate genuine, life-giving relationships with integrity, respect, and honor? Do you have roommates who see the real you and know what you're like when your guard is down and you're exhausted? The quality of those relationships is a great indicator.

That's how shepherds roll.

4. LOOK AT THE SHEEP.

The sheep are the people God has entrusted to your care whether you're a lead pastor, an associate, on the worship team, in student ministry, kids, production, or anywhere else. If you serve and represent the church, you're caring for sheep.

I need to make a critical point of clarification here, especially if God's really been speaking to you and you're passionate about making some changes. Jesus didn't use the sheep and shepherd metaphor because He literally wanted us to identify with these animals. He did it because it was something people saw every day and they were familiar with.

Therefore, we follow His pattern. You're coming to the end of an extensive, in-depth study into the language and concept of sheep and shepherds in the Bible. The people in your church probably haven't been thinking about it at all. Most of them don't know it's in the Bible.

In your enthusiasm, don't overuse the term "shepherd," don't regularly refer to the people as sheep, and don't change names or programs in your church to things like "flocks" or "herds." The same way those things were meaningful to an agricultural society in the ancient world, most of those concepts are lost on the people we serve (unless you live in a farming community!).

It would be tragically ironic to overuse sheep language in a way that makes them feel more anxious and insecure. That's not a win.

I KNOW HOW THE PEOPLE I'M RESPONSIBLE FOR THINK. I KNOW WHAT THEY CARE ABOUT. THAT'S WHAT IT MEANS TO BE A SHEPHERD. THAT'S THE POINT.

They're into things like purpose, calling, destiny, significance, fulfillment, personal growth, and development. They're suburban, goal-driven, ambitious, upwardly mobile, and very preoccupied with the future success of their children.

But they're also lacking some things. They wish they had more peace. They're struggling to find significance and meaning in their overcrowded, super-busy lives. They want a stronger relationship with their spouse and their kids.

Human nature has not changed. The Bible is as powerful and meaningful today as when it was first written. But the language and the metaphors we use are adaptable to fully communicate the intended meaning through the guiding presence of the Holy Spirit, who leads and guides us into all truth.

The way we shepherd the sheep is to love and serve them—to help them grow in their relationship with God. We know they need help learning to study and confess God's Word, to develop a prayer life, and to build their faith. But what they really want is to experience God's love and presence, to make a friend, to have a stronger marriage, and to get help raising their kids.

That's what they're into. And that's where we're leading them.

5. LOOK AT YOUR TEAMS.

All four of the previous points build on each other. But if you're at the place in your journey where the most pressing challenge you have is growth, this is the most important one. However, no matter how bad you want to grow, if you skip the other four, you're going to end up making things worse for yourself.

Don't try to be a rancher without being a shepherd.

I'm a rancher. There are thousands of people I don't have regular direct responsibility over (beyond preaching and casting vision), but I love the sheep. I don't shepherd shepherds because I'm frustrated with sheep. I do it because it's the most effective way to build the flock and grow the herds.

Teams of shepherds can care for lots of sheep when they have great communication, trust, clear vision, and an intentional culture. This means you have to regularly spend time talking to each other. Ministry is so busy, if we're not careful, we spend all our time working *in* it (accomplishing the necessary tasks) without ever working *on* it (evaluating our processes and strategies).

If you're leading a team, honor your team members when they're willing to be courageously honest with you. This doesn't mean you have to agree, but don't yell at them and don't be unnecessarily rough with them. Remind them the fence is there for a reason. Trust and relational capital are two of your most valuable resources.

I hope all of our teams, in all of our departments, at all of our campuses—and whatever it looks like in your context—will grow as both sheep and shepherds.

My prayer through this journey, the thing I get most excited about, is the restoration of growing, biblical, visionary churches that love and care for their people well. Where kindness exceeds expectations, where the next steps are clear, and where everyone from the lead pastor to the newest guest is growing.

Thank you for going on this journey. I have a new appreciation for how important this shift in perspective is. I believe God is doing something in us.

I'm keenly aware I'm not the Chief Shepherd—but I know for certain I can be the shepherd He created me to be. That's all He's asking of me.

I don't know about you, but I'm grateful for a target I can hit.

Few things are more frustrating than trying to get motivated every day when you don't feel like you're winning. I talk to way too many pastors who are consistently discouraged. They got into this because they love Jesus and they want to make a difference, but most days, they wonder what they're doing with their lives.

I know what that feels like. I've been there. But we don't have to stay there.

Let me encourage you—your Great Shepherd sees you and loves you. He's given you everything you need. He's not asking you to be anyone other than who He made you.

You don't have to be famous.

You don't have to be the main speaker at the conference.

You don't have to go viral.

You don't need a gimmick.

You don't need to come up with some deep spiritual insight no one has ever heard.

You don't need to move to a new city.

You don't need a new role on the team.

Right now, exactly where you're at, you can absolutely hit the target He gave you: **"Take care of My sheep."**

And as another shepherd under our Chief Shepherd, I add my voice of encouragement to His. I'm cheering you on. You're making an impact. Every time you love and serve God's people, you're hitting the bullseye.

You're crushing it for the Kingdom.

More than the powerful messages you preach, the meaningful moments of worship, or the incredible times we experience together, the people remember how you made them feel.

I try to make this as practical and as tangible as possible.

- **Write a note to your spouse or your child.**
- **Send a text to the team member who's giving their all.**
- **Have the conversation you've been avoiding.**
- **Create that experience for the person you love.**
- **Give that generous gift.**
- **Tell someone's story that makes you cry and moves your heart.**

These things aren't always celebrated. They don't seem like that big of a deal. They don't always instantly produce what we expect. But these small acts of service end up producing big fruit in our lives.

It's how we win with people.

At the time I'm writing this, last weekend we had more people in church than ever before, in more rooms, at more campuses. When I first started, I had no idea this would be what it looks like.

Honestly, it's more people than I ever thought I would preach to. When you're young, you think about that kind of moment. You imagine, *If I could just get there, I'll feel like I've arrived.*

Take it from someone who was just there, here's what happened: Moments before the lights went up to start the last service of the weekend, Jesus spoke to me. Everything else may have changed, but His message did not.

He said the same thing: *Jeff, make sure you tell them I love them.*

That's our target. We can hit it. Let's do it together.

KEY TAKEAWAYS

CHAPTER 12

! You can win with people. Your whole church can. You can come back to the call Jesus entrusted to His first followers: the call to shepherd people.

! **What Do I Do Now?**

1. Start with you.
2. Come back to the issue of calling.
3. Let's talk family.
4. Look at the sheep.
5. Look at your teams.

! You're a sheep. Jesus is your Shepherd. We love because HE first loved us.

! Before we use our gifts to serve others, before we respond to His calling, before we can minister to anyone else, He ministers to us.

! The way we shepherd the sheep is to love and serve them—to help them grow in their relationship with God.

! Teams of shepherds can care for lots of sheep when they have great communication, trust, clear vision, and an intentional culture.

KEY TAKEAWAYS

CHAPTER 12

!

Your Great Shepherd sees you and loves you. He's given you everything you need. He's not asking you to be anyone other than who He made you.

!

Small acts of service end up producing big fruit in our lives:

- Write a note to your spouse or your child.
- Send a text to the team member who's giving their all.
- Have the conversation you've been avoiding.
- Create that experience for the person you love.
- Give that generous gift.
- Tell someone's story that makes you cry and moves your heart.

CHAPTER 12

Win Today, Win Tomorrow

DISCUSSION

1. How does prioritizing your relationship with Jesus shape your leadership and calling?

2. How has your understanding of calling changed through this journey? What do you see differently now about your role in ministry?

3. What specific actions can you take to foster trust, communication, and clear vision within your team?

CHAPTER 12

Win Today, Win Tomorrow

APPLICATION

1. **Personal Reflection:** Reflect on two important connections in your life:

   A. How is your relationship with Jesus? Are you allowing Him to shepherd you fully, or have you been operating on auto-pilot?

   B. How well are you prioritizing family right now? Are there any changes you need to make?

2. **Action Step:** Identify two or three people in your life to serve this week.

   A. Determine what you will do this week to help them feel what you feel. Consider the list on page 206 as a starting place.

NOTES

Introduction

1 Donald A. McGavran and George G. Hunter, III, ed. Lyle Schaller, *Church Growth: Strategies That Work* (Nashville: Abingdon, 1980), 90-91.

CHAPTER 1 | Why Do We Need to Win with People?

1 This is a paraphrase of a quote often attributed to Mark Twain.

2 2 Timothy 1:9

3 Romans 12:6-8

4 Psalm 75:6-7

5 1 Peter 5:8

6 Psalm 23:1

7 Psalm 78:52; 95:7; 100:3

8 John 10:14

9 1 Peter 5:2-4; Acts 20:28

10 1 Kings 19

11 Mark 6:7-13

12 Matthew 14:22-33

13 Matthew 16:13-20

14 Mark 14:27-31, 66-72

CHAPTER 2 | Shepherds Smell Like Sheep

1 Luke 19:10

2 Luke 15:3-7

3 Matthew 14:22-31; Matthew 16:13-23; Luke 22:31-32; Mark 14:27-31, 66-72

4 Acts 2:14-41

5 Acts 5:1-11

6 See Acts 6 and 7

CHAPTER 3 | God's Heart for People (His Sheep)

1 Jim Davis and Michael Graham with Ryan P. Burge, *The Great Dechurching: Who's Leaving, Why Are They Going, And What Will It Take to Bring Them Back?* (Grand Rapids: Zondervan, 2023), 125.

2 Canadian Sheep Federation and The National Farm Animal Council, "Code of Practice for the Care and Handling of Sheep," 2013, https://www.nfacc.ca/sheep-code.

3 Dallas Willard, *Life Without Lack: Living in the Fullness of Psalm 23* (Grand Rapids: Zondervan, 2018), 186-187.

4 Kenneth Bailey, *The Good Shepherd: A Thousand-Year Journey from Psalm 23 to the New Testament* (Downers Grove: InterVarsity Press, 2014), 13.

5 Bailey, *The Good Shepherd*, 31-65.

6 David Gibson, *The Lord of Psalm 23: Jesus Our Shepherd, Companion, and Host* (Wheaton: Crossway, 2023), 121.

7 John 1:29

CHAPTER 4 | Jesus, the Chief Shepherd

1 Psalm 78:52; Isaiah 40:11

2 Psalm 79:13; 100:3

3 David in Psalm 78:70-72; Moses in Isaiah 63:11

4 Micah 5:4

5 Daniel 7:13-14

6 Jeremiah 23:1-4; 50:6

7 See Exodus 2:11-12; Numbers 20:11-12, Exodus 32:19-20, and 2 Samuel 11, among others

8 2 Samuel 12

9 Ezekiel 34

10 John 10:1

11 John 10:7

12 John 10:3

13 John 10:5

14 John 10:4
15 Matthew 10:5-6
16 Luke 15:3-6
17 Bailey, *The Good Shepherd,* 44.
18 Bailey, *The Good Shepherd,* 49.

CHAPTER 5 | The Call to the Shepherd's Life

1 Ephesians 1:5; John 1:12; 1 Peter 4:10
2 Matthew 28:18-20
3 Ephesians 4:11-13
4 1 Peter 5:2
5 Mark 6:7
6 Acts 5:1-11
7 Matthew 9:36
8 Luke 9:62

CHAPTER 6 | Practical Ways Your Church Can Win with People

1 Matthew 14:14-21
2 Dale Carnegie, *How to Win Friends and Influence People* (New York: Simon & Schuster, 1981).
3 Carnegie, *How to Win Friends,* 63-70.
4 Acts 2:46
5 Will Guidara, *Unreasonable Hospitality: The Remarkable Power of Giving People More Than They Expect* (New York: Optimism Press, 2022), 22.
6 Aaron Earls, "The Surprising Reason Most People Choose a Church," Lifeway Research, April 20, 2017, https://research.lifeway.com/2017/04/20/surprising-reason-people-choose-church/.
7 David Brooks, *How to Know a Person: The Art of Seeing Others Deeply and Being Deeply Seen* (New York: Random House Large Print, 2023), 12.
8 This quote has been attributed to Maya Angelou, Carl W. Bueher, and others.

CHAPTER 7 | The Shepherd's Most Important Challenge

1 Hebrews 4:13
2 Henry Cloud, *Boundaries for Leaders: Results, Relationships, and Being Ridiculously in Charge* (New York: HarperCollins Publishers, 2013), 14.
3 Kevin Lehman and Bill Pentak, *The Way of the Shepherd: Seven Secrets to Managing Productive People* (Grand Rapids: Zondervan, 2004), 99-100.
4 Charles Haddon Spurgeon, "On Humbling Ourselves Before God," The Spurgeon Center, January 1, 1970, https://www.spurgeon.org/resource-library/sermons/on-humbling-ourselves-before-god/#flipbook/.
5 See John 21:20-22 among others
6 Genesis 3:8
7 Acts 20:28
8 1 Timothy 4:16
9 2 Corinthians 13:5
10 Romans 5:8
11 1 John 4:19
12 1 John 4:8
13 Proverbs 29:1, 11
14 Matthew 9:37-38
15 Malcolm Gladwell, *Outliers: The Story of Success* (New York: Hachette Book Group, 2008), 39-47.

CHAPTER 8 | Win with Your Team

1 Matthew 9:37-38
2 John 15:8
3 1 Thessalonians 1:6-10

CHAPTER 9 | How to Help the Herd Win

1 Genesis 2:18
2 Proverbs 17:17
3 Proverbs 13:20
4 Philippians 4:19

5 2 Peter 1:3

6 William Shakespeare, *Julius Caesar*, Ed. by Roma Gill (Oxford: Oxford University Press, 2001).

7 ESV

CHAPTER 10 | Protecting Your Winning Culture

1 1 Samuel 17:32-37

2 Matthew 10:16; Luke 10:3

3 1 Timothy 4:6-7

4 Colossians 2:2-3

5 2 Timothy 2:24-26

6 Timothy Witmer, *The Shepherd Leader: Achieving Effective Shepherding in Your Church* (Phillipsburg: P&R Publishing Company, 2010), 178.

7 Matthew 16:18

CHAPTER 11 | The Multi-Dimensional Shepherd

1 McGavran, Hunter, III, Schaller, *Church Growth: Strategies That Work*, 90-91.

2 Matthew 11:19

3 1 Timothy 4:15

4 Matthew 16:18

5 John 21:17

6 Acts 1:4, 8

CHAPTER 12 | Win Today, Win Tomorrow

1 1 John 4:19

2 Romans 5:8

MORE FROM
JEFF LITTLE

LEADTOWIN.COM

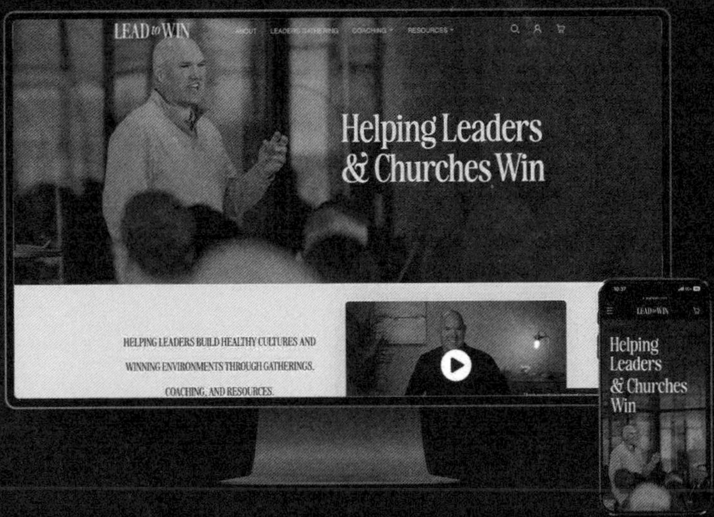
LEAD to WIN
ABOUT
LEADERS GATHERING
COACHING
RESOURCES
Helping Leaders & Churches Win
HELPING LEADERS BUILD HEALTHY CULTURES AND WINNING ENVIRONMENTS THROUGH GATHERINGS, COACHING, AND RESOURCES.
Helping Leaders & Churches Win

Find Messages and Ways to Connect

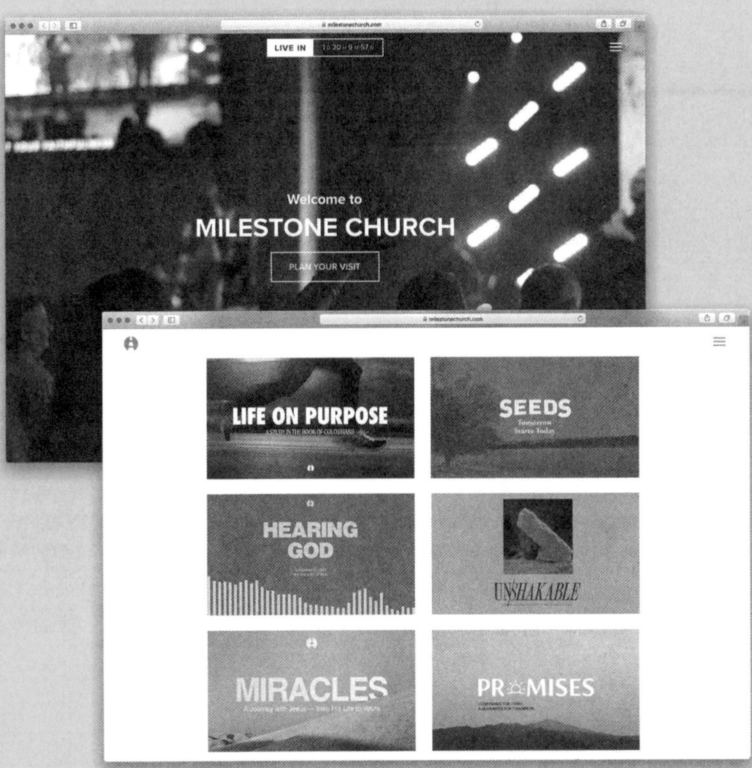

MILESTONECHURCH.COM

CONNECT WITH

JEFF LITTLE

@PASTORJEFFLITTLE

@JEFFLITTLE